James Jorgensen

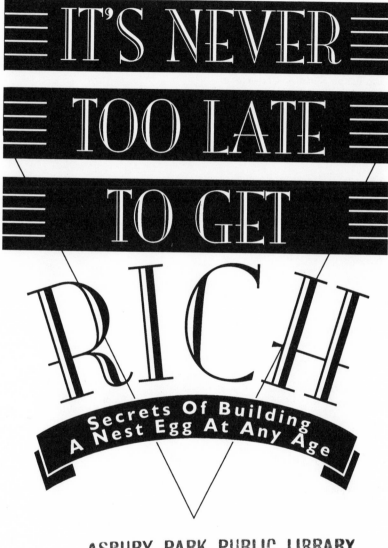

IT'S NEVER TOO LATE TO GET RICH

Secrets Of Building A Nest Egg At Any Age

Dearborn
Financial Publishing, Inc.

While a great deal of care has been taken to provide accurate and current information, the ideas, suggestions, general principles and conclusions presented in this text are subject to local, state and federal laws and regulations, court cases and any revisions of same. The reader is thus urged to consult legal counsel regarding any points of law—this publication should not be used as a substitute for competent legal advice.

Publisher: Kathleen A. Welton
Associate Editor: Karen A. Christensen
Senior Project Editor: Jack L. Kiburz
Editorial Assistant: Kristen G. Landreth
Cover Design: Jenkins Corporation

Published by Dearborn Financial Publishing, Inc.

Printed in the United States of America

94 95 96 10 9 8 7 6 5 4 3 2 1

Library of Congress Cataloging-in-Publication Data

Jorgensen, James A.
    It's never too late to get rich : secrets of building a nest egg
at any age / James Jorgensen.
        p. cm.
    Includes index.
    ISBN 0–7931–0952–3 (hard)
    1. Finance, Personal.   2. Saving and investment.   3. Retirement–
United States–Planning.   4. Baby-boom generation–Finance,
Personal.   5. Parents–Finance, Personal.   6. College costs.
I. Title.
HG179.J633   1994
332.024′01–dc20   94–9009
                                                              CIP

*This book is dedicated to my lifelong
companion, my wonderful wife
Patricia*

Other Books by James Jorgensen

The Graying of America
Your Retirement Income
How To Stay Ahead in the Money Game
How To Make IRAs Work for You
MoneyShock

ACKNOWLEDGMENTS

Writing a book like this requires help from a lot of people. I especially want to thank Richard Shelton, president of California Investment Trust, who gave me help on mutual funds, George Gordon, President of Western Annuity in San Francisco, who gave me insight into retirement plans, and James King, CFP, Walnut Creek, California, who assisted me in the study of financial planners. A number of experts also checked the technical content of the book and helped me with the chapters on credit cards and resources. I also want to thank Louisa Arndt at **It's Your Money** for her help in making the book more friendly to the reader.

CONTENTS

The Old Rules Still Work

*T*he temperature had risen to 97 degrees in the forenoon. I could tell it was going to be another sizzler because the black repair tar in the center of the street had already begun to melt. I walked over to the five-cent Coke machine and took out a bottle. The farmers were talking about the new tractors, the hay rakes and money. I drew closer to listen to their words, not because I was interested in learning anything about hay rakes, but because I knew these farmers always had money. And money in my youth was a precious commodity.

I grew up in a small farming community in the San Joaquin valley in California and worked my way through high school. My father was an accountant for a farm implement firm, and he walked to work. So, in a small town where most people used their feet, I often walked down to the shop and talked with the farmers. It was easy to tell the farmers from the tractor salesmen; the farmers all wore bib overalls. They were the garment of choice because they had large pockets, you could hang tools around your waist, and they allowed for an ever-larger tummy that ample farm food tended to produce. Not just any overalls, mind you. The correct pair, as far as I could tell, had the logo "Oshkosh B'Gosh" sewn on the top flap. Beneath the label were the magic words "The Genuine Article."

What I learned in high school about building wealth and managing personal finances came not from the classroom, but from the farmers. At first glance, they did not appear to be sophisticated investors or money managers, which they weren't, but they always paid cash, drove big Cadillacs and knew the value of a dollar saved. It's possible, of course, that the farmers learned from Benjamin Franklin, who in 1758 said, "For age and want save while you may; no morning sun lasts a whole day."

I didn't realize the importance of the basic money management principles I learned over a bottle of Coke and a set of bib overalls until I set off for the University of California's business school to learn what I thought were the latest words on how to make money. I graduated from the university, having taken all the required business courses, but I was still left with the problem that, no matter how much I learned, I still couldn't make money on money I didn't have.

Now, looking back over 30 years as a corporate executive in marketing, a stockbroker, a financial planner, author, radio talk show host, newsletter writer and syndicated newspaper columnist, it's clear to me that whatever I needed to know about becoming wealthy I learned from the farmers in my youth. When it came to providing financial security and wealth, they were indeed "the genuine article."

Today, as I read my mail and listen to questions from my radio audience and from participants at my seminars, I sense on a very personal level the concerns of many people over finding the money to build a realistic nest egg and keeping it safe once they have invested it. They are scared about the future, feel they are falling behind financially, worried about their debt and unsure of what to do next.

Most of the questions I get on the radio are from listeners whose financial life is not working out as they planned. My answer to these concerns—and the motivation behind writing this book—

is the firm conviction that, amidst the worry and anxiety, there is much the individual can do to build and protect his or her financial security. I believe that anyone who is willing to make the effort can understand basic money management techniques.

The problem today is not where to invest, but how to sock away some money each month so we have something to invest. We are a nation of spenders, not savers. Relying on credit cards in the race to live the good life, millions of Americans have buried themselves under a mountain of bills. Most baby boomers, those in their thirties, forties and fifties, simply aren't saving enough money to meet the so-called "triple squeeze": the costs of college, health care and retirement. And if you are a baby boomer born in 1950, for example, your average lifetime tax rate will be a whopping one-third higher than that of your parents.

For most baby boomers, it's a case of denial. A recent study concluded that baby boomers, on average, save only 34 percent of what they'll need to retire at age 65 and maintain their standard of living. One reason, say retirement planners, is that they have an exaggerated opinion of what their company pension will be worth, and they're kidding themselves into believing they have lots of time to save for both retirement and family emergencies. In fact, the pension gravy train has left the station, and the responsibility for retirement security is quickly being transferred from the employer to the working individual.

A recent issue of the *New Yorker* featured a cartoon depicting a well-dressed couple standing on a street corner, tin cup in hand, with a sign reading: "Not as well off as our parents were at our age."

According to the U.S. Census Bureau, there are about 50 million baby boomers in this country, and more than half of them, according to a Gallup poll, are worried that they will run out of money before they run out of breath. They are often referred to as the "sandwich generation," squeezed between caring for themselves, their children and their parents. During the past 20 years, those who did invest made hefty double-digit returns in the stock market, often investing in mutual funds that didn't exist in the 1960s, and they found the door open to personal savings with individual retirement accounts and, later, 401(k) company savings plans.

In 1972, stock funds made up 93 percent of all mutual fund assets. A $10,000 investment in stocks in 1972 could now be worth about $65,000. In 1994, with the market's spasms giving many investors the jitters, stock funds accounted for only 28 percent of the total, with low-yielding money market funds accounting for 38 percent and bond funds 34 percent.

The path to prosperity has taken a new twist, but, as evidenced by the rush into money market and bond funds, most investors haven't learned the lesson: Those who keep their money safe, obsessed by fears of the Great Depression and afraid to take any risks, will miss out on the windfall of the 1990s. *The greatest lesson of the past is that "safe" investments are at greater risk than most of us realize.*

While it's true that safe money market accounts or insured certificates of deposit will shelter you from the gyrations of the stock market, this safety exposes you to an even greater peril: the rapid decline of the purchasing power of your assets.

The truth is, if you want to become wealthy in the future, you have to shake off the mistakes of the past, be willing to take some risks with equity investments in a growing America, spend less, save more and continue to educate yourself in modern financial planning. Those who believe they can keep their money growing in a risk-free greenhouse will end up in the poorhouse.

Now a word from the real world: You're not a young person any more, and riding off into the sunset isn't going to be any easier in the years to come. If you plan to live happily ever after, you'll need to stick to a serious long-term savings and investment plan. And you need to start now. Otherwise, as you near retirement you may find that your cash box is almost empty, and you'll have to depend on Social Security in the best years of your life.

What's more, Social Security won't be much help in the future. Many people who have paid Social Security taxes their entire working lives will wake up tomorrow with hangovers that won't fit in the overhead bin. Dorcas R. Hardy, former commissioner of Social Security, tells me that the Social Security trust fund is more myth than reality. She says, "Baby boomers should think of Social Security benefits as a true 'floor of protection' at best, and not plan for anywhere near the largess their parents received." The new data on the Social Security payback of all taxes and interest earned indicate that a worker retiring in 1980 received back his or her entire lifetime contribution in less than four years. Retirees in 1993, who have paid much higher taxes for a longer period of time, may have to wait 14 years for a full payback. In 2015, the payback is estimated to be 25 years, long after many retirees are no longer living.

Social Security will also hit high earners hard with far less in benefits for the taxes they've paid. In 1993, a typical 65-year-old retiree and spouse whose 1992 earnings were only $20,000 might receive $1,125 a month, while an individual with more than $50,000 of income might receive only $1,625 a month. Don't think you can beat the game by going back to work. Those under age 65 who collect Social Security benefits lose $1 of benefits for every $2 they earn on the job over $8,040 a year. Between ages 65 and 69, retirees lose $1 of benefits for every $3 they earn over $11,160 a year. Those over age 70 who continue to work have no earnings test. These are 1994 limits, and they are adjusted for inflation each year.

And now for the really grim news: Hardy says, "If 65 was the proper retirement age in 1940, the comparable age to begin receiving Social Security benefits today, reflecting remaining life expectancy, should be at least 73." Congress started this trend in 1983, when it increased retirement ages. Anyone born before 1938 can still retire on full benefits at age 65. The retirement age moves up two months each year for those born between 1943 and 1954 who retire at age 66, and those born in 1960 or later will retire at age 67. Hardy believes Congress should not use the "drip system" of gradually increasing the retirement age and tell the public that in the future the normal retirement date will be age 70.

Because people are living longer, and it's costing Social Security billions of dollars each year in extra monthly checks the system didn't count on a decade or two ago, major changes will occur in the future. Not only will the normal retirement age rise, but beneficiaries will face a means test to collect the retirement benefits. The plan is to cut back or eliminate benefits to retirees based on their income levels. For example, a retiree with $40,000 of income, not counting Social Security benefits, might lose most or all of the retirement benefits. What Congress is looking at, says Hardy, is that by 2016, if no major changes are made in taxes or benefits, Social Security will have a cash deficit of $13 billion. By 2021, $200 billion, and by 2030, $700 billion.

You'll also need more assets to tide you over until you reach retirement age. Today, if you start receiving benefits early, at age 62, Social Security will give you the equivalent of financial sticker shock. If you qualify for $800 a month at age 65 and retire with a spouse, the benefit would be $1,200 a month, but if you retire early at age 62 with a spouse, the benefit would be only $790 a month.

The clock is also ticking for baby boomers who don't start saving each month. The reason is, as we'll discover later in this book, that a dollar saved today can be worth $15, even $25, a month in retirement. On the other hand, later in life, saving $15 or $20 may provide only a dollar a month more after retirement.

The good news is that the basic building blocks of financial wealth have remained unchanged. Anyone, regardless of income or age, can start immediately building wealth with a few simple lifestyle changes. The secret is to follow the rules and let time make you rich. In each chapter, I've outlined the basic rules you need to follow. If I've done my job as an author, you'll learn why certain people have a comfortable retirement and others try to make do on Social Security.

As you read this book, remember these eight rules for financial success:

1. Establish a Budget
2. Pay Off Your Personal Debt
3. Pay Yourself First
4. Buy Adequate Insurance
5. Safeguard the Money You've Already Saved
6. Take Advantage of Your Employer's Retirement Plan
7. Be Willing To Accept Some Risk
8. Keep Your Hands Off Your Investments

These are my golden rules for financial success. Think positive— if you follow the rules, you will get rich. They are guaranteed to work if you follow them each day. On the other hand, this is not a "get-rich-quick" book, or a "doom-and-gloom" book to scare you into believing that the next market crash or depression is just around the corner. It is a book on the basics of personal money management and building wealth.

I am talking about the pit in your stomach that tells you each day that you're living from paycheck to paycheck, that your personal finances resemble a bowl of spaghetti in mid-explosion and that building a sizable nest egg continues to remain beyond your grasp. Again, the good news is that if you follow the rules in this book in your investing and your money management, you'll accomplish what you need to become wealthy. Are the rules easy to follow? Yes! Most Americans who retire on a monthly Social Security check could retire rich—if they knew and followed these basic rules.

What I'm about to tell you in this book comes from years of watching people accumulate wealth: how they manage the money they already have and spend each month, how they consistently earn double-digit returns and why what they do with their money is as important as the money they save. You'll also learn for the first time that most of what you hear on television or read in the newspapers about investing is nothing more than "hype" to help the brokers or mutual funds do business.

My intent is that this book will cover only what you need to know to become wealthy, including the best time-tested advice I can give you and my general philosophy of investing, which has evolved from years of working and talking with people across America. My office is littered with personal finance books from authors who want to tell readers how to invest in the stock market, how to get rich, how to outguess the market, but they all assume that you already have the money and simply don't know how to invest it. Many of these books, with their high-risk ideas, assume you don't want to sleep at night. They also assume that you want to learn every detail of how they will make you rich. I've tried to cut out the stuff that's not important and concentrate on what I think you need to learn and do in your busy life. I haven't covered every possible investment, option or tax law because I've also assumed that you don't want to make investing your money a full-time job.

Before you get ready to learn how to manage and invest your money, let me tell you this: One of the hardest rules for people to accept and the most overlooked basic fact is that becoming wealthy today is incredibly easy. It's boring, but it's easy if you stick to a plan and follow the basic rules. Perhaps because it is so simple, most people can't do it. This may sound a little goofy, but it's true.

To find out why, let's meet the people in the bib overalls.

CHAPTER 1

Basic Rules for Financial Success

*F*or many people, financial planning has turned into waiting for the phone to ring. "Hello, I want to tell you your Uncle Henry just died and left you $5 million." While this may be a typical fantasy of anxious mid-lifers, it's also the most common way our financial ship hits the shoals. We spend, we dream, we wait for Uncle Henry's money, and then we find at the end of the month that there's nothing left to save. Here are some shocking facts: Nearly half the employees eligible for their company's 401(k) plan don't contribute anything. More than 70 percent of all working Americans don't have even a modest emergency fund to tide them over if they lose their job or can't work.

What's even worse is being addicted to buying on credit. Consider this scenario: You take a vacation to the surf and sand, putting it all on your credit card. When you get back home, you receive a statement with $5,000 of new debt. You are too embarrassed to get a bank loan, so you opt for less paperwork and pay the 18 percent interest on the credit card. Now consider this: If you make only the minimum payment each month, by the time the $5,000 is paid off, the cost of your vacation will have more than doubled.

The bankruptcy rolls are filled with middle-class baby boomers with big-time credit card debt. Without the memory of the Great Depression of earlier generations, they use their credit cards based on expected earnings. When they get a pink slip and face unemployment, the once-manageable credit card payment turns into a monster that can quickly devour their savings.

One suggestion for cutting impulse spending comes from the National Center for Financial Education (NCFE), a nonprofit organization dedicated to helping people do a better job of spending and saving their money. NCFE says that people need to practice "safe spending." To help, they offer a credit card "condom," which slips over the card and carries a warning to the overextended user. "Keep this condom cover over your credit card. The few seconds it takes to get the card ready for use can reduce the urge to spend, spend, spend, and then you'll have money to invest." (National Center for Financial Education, Box 34070, San Diego, CA 92163, 619-232-8811.)

Once you are no longer a "chargeaholic" with pockets full of credit cards, running up higher and higher balances, you'll find saving money is like finding a gold mine right in your paycheck.

A lot of people have no idea where their money is going and get caught in a never-ending trap:

- If they spend too much, they can't save.
- If they can't save, they can't invest.
- If they can't invest, they end up broke.

People often give the most imaginative reasons for spending now and delaying savings, but statistics don't lie. The Social Security Administration says that 13 percent of all retirees have no other income but their monthly benefit checks. Another 24 percent rely on Social Security for 90 percent or more of their total income in retirement. In fact, without Social Security benefits, more than half the people age 65 or older would have incomes below the poverty level.

If you think you can live on Social Security benefits when you turn 65, consider this 1993 table from the Social Security Administration.

	Estimated Monthly Benefits	
Current		*Worker and*
Annual Income	*Single Worker*	*Nonworking Spouse*
$20,000	$ 750	$1,125
30,000	916	1,375
40,000	1,000	1,500
50,000	1,083	1,625

If you're counting on Social Security to provide the lion's share of your retirement income, you'll be in for an unpleasant surprise if your annual income is much above the national average. The worth of any retirement plan is its *replacement ratio*—that is, the percentage of your last working salary the plan will provide. The Social Security replacement ratio falls dramatically as income increases. If your current annual income is $15,000, Social Security will replace about 50 percent at age 65; at $25,000, about 42 percent; at $40,000, about 30 percent; and for those who earn more than $50,000 a year, only about 24 percent or less. And, as I write this book, the suits on Capitol Hill tell me plans are already under way in Congress to cut the replacement ratio further to around 18 to 20 percent for those who earn more than $50,000 a year.

To find out how much Social Security can bankroll your retirement, call 800-772-1213 or visit the nearest office to obtain the Personal Earnings and Benefits Estimate Statement (Form SSA-7004). Complete the form, mail it to Social Security, and you'll receive a yearly breakdown of salary credited to your account and an estimate of benefits if you retire or become disabled.

Basic Rule #1:

Save 10 percent of your income first.

This is the most important rule in the book. It will give you the means to retire with a comfortable living, help your kids with college expenses and find the good things of life.

"Save 10 percent of my income first? Impossible!" you say. "Not with my bills and expenses." You are not alone in that belief. But if you want to achieve financial success without Uncle Henry or the lottery, you must save part of what you earn each month. Is it easy to do? Well, it's not as easy as giving in to the temptation of easy credit, but it's easier than you think.

A farmer once told me, "Look, sonny, if you don't pay yourself first, no one else will."

"Is that how you got rich?" I asked.

"That's it," he said, pulling on his bib overalls. "Lord knows you don't have to be smart, but if you don't save your money, all the fancy investment advice in the world won't make you rich."

"How did you learn to pay yourself first?" I asked.

"The problem most people face is that they can't pay themselves first because no one has sent them a bill. To get started, I made up a bunch of bills, put them in envelopes addressed to me and gave them to a friend. Each month, I got a bill in the mail and sent the money back to the bank. After a while, I just included those bills with my mortgage and other payments, and I never missed the money."

Most of us already have experience with paying ourselves first. It's called *forced savings*. When we buy a life insurance policy or a new home, we are forced to save to meet the required payments.

If you want to reduce your overall spending so that you can pay yourself first and have enough left to pay your monthly bills and expenses, follow the lead of the wealthy. They don't need to make a statement as to who they are; they buy only what they need and travel with battered luggage.

Here are some ways you can save each month after paying yourself first:

1. Rent videos instead of going to the movies.
2. Make a list before you go to the grocery store, and stick to it. Shop at supermarkets, not convenience stores.

3. Shop the sales, and shop early while the bargains are available. Find the manufacturer-owned outlet stores at one of the hundreds of factory outlet centers across the nation. They often sell their branded goods at up to 50 percent off department store prices.

4. Instead of a new car, buy a one- or two-year-old car in mint condition with low mileage and the balance of the factory warranty. You can save 40 percent off the new car price, sometimes $10,000 to $15,000, and a mechanic can check out the car for less than $100. To save money, you can also lease a used car from Ford Motor Credit or General Motors' GMAC. These are two-year-old cars that themselves were leased when new and come with low mileage and the balance of the factory warranty.

5. Take your lunch to work instead of buying it. At $6 a lunch per day, that can save you about $125 a month, or $1,500 a year.

6. Save a dollar of change a day. That's $365 a year.

7. Avoid buying on credit and wasting your money on interest. If you do buy on credit, apply for a low-interest credit card. The average credit card user can save between $100 and $150 a year in interest with a low-interest card.

8. Refinance your mortgage. With today's low interest rates, people who purchased a home a few years ago can cut their monthly payments by as much as 20 percent.

9. Shop "little-used" clothing stores.

10. Always buy big-ticket items out of season. Buy an air conditioner when it's cold outside, have your new roof put on in the summer, and shop end-of-season promotions, which can slash prices as much as 50 percent when merchants want to clear out their inventory.

You won't be lowering your standard of living or depriving yourself by following these simple suggestions. All you will be doing is saving money. That means you can start paying yourself first and increase the contributions to your savings accounts and retirement plans.

Basic Rule #2:

Don't lose money.

This might sound like a silly rule, but if you want to become wealthy, you can't afford to lose money. In my 30 years in the financial planning area, I've found that most people do lose money. The reason? They are looking for an easy route to riches without understanding how they are investing their hard-earned money, or by trusting the wrong people who tell them what they want to believe. The more they try to make money in rotten business deals, hot stock tips and high-yielding schemes, the more money they lose. I know this is the exciting way to put your money to work, but you have to decide if you want excitement or wealth.

Even without losing money, only about 20 percent of the Americans born in the baby boom years between 1946 and 1964 are socking away enough money to retire anywhere near their current standard of living. The older baby boomers, those born between 1946 and 1956, will need to triple their savings rate just to maintain their standard of living after they turn 65. Just how important that income will be is shown by the fact that today about 70 percent of married people ages 51 to 61 have four-generation families— themselves, an elderly parent and children who have children of their own. Another 25 percent have three-generation families. In years to come, today's couples probably will need to give financial assistance to their children and their parents.

One way to motivate yourself to start a savings plan and stick to it is to have a specific goal. Whatever the goals may be—saving for college, a new car, a new home or retirement—set up separate accounts, just like a bank, and add to them each month. That way, you'll know exactly what you're aiming for and why you are paying yourself first while the markdowns run wild at the local department store.

It's not how much money you make each month that counts, it's how you manage the money. Scores of credit counseling services tell the same story—people with annual incomes of $150,000 don't have a dime in the bank and are past due on their bills. If you save part of your income each month, you can become wealthy without earning a hefty salary.

Basic Rule #3:

Learn the importance of compounding.

Have you ever wondered how some of America's greatest fortunes were made? They were made, in large part, by the magic of compound interest. It's true that these early millionaires avoided income taxes and often made business deals without regard for the public good, but once they had the money, it was compound interest that made them wealthy. Today, the same principle is at work in your individual retirement accounts and your company retirement plans.

To make compounding work you need discipline to save, perseverance to continue to save and, most of all, time. People who have become wealthy on their own have already learned how to use the magic of compounding.

The secret of compounding: You not only earn interest income on your original investment, but you also earn interest on your interest. What most people overlook in saving long term for retirement security is that the second half of the equation is more important than the first.

Think of compounding in terms of riding a bicycle. An insured certificate of deposit yielding 5 percent is like riding a bicycle with a tire that is gradually losing air. After a time, you'll feel like you're riding on the rim. With a bond fund yielding 10 percent, you're riding a sturdy American-built bicycle that will deliver the goods. With a good-performing stock mutual fund returning 15 percent a year, you're riding a lightweight foreign bike that will speed your way toward retirement.

If you invest $1,000 and never add to your initial investment, here's how compounding can build your original nest egg with the time value of money:

End of Year	5%	10%	15%
5	$1,276	$1,610	$ 2,011
10	1,628	2,594	4,046
15	2,079	4,117	8,137
20	2,653	6,727	16,367

This table also illustrates the value of investing in stock mutual funds. With an average annual total return of around 15 percent, stocks can build your nest egg over 20 years six times faster than a 5 percent savings account.

If you can invest $1,000 each year in an IRA or 401(k) retirement plan, the compounding effect pushes into high gear.

End of Year	Total Invested	5%	10%	15%
5	$ 5,000	$ 5,802	$ 6,716	$ 7,754
10	10,000	13,207	17,531	23,349
15	15,000	22,657	34,950	54,717
20	20,000	34,719	63,002	117,810

Over time, the interest rate or income you earn on your investments is very important. In this example, at the end of 20 years, as the interest rate doubles so does the size of the nest egg. You can call this long-term way of earning money "tortoise investing." Like a tortoise, compounding takes time to cross the road, but with its steady progress, it will reach its goal. "Jackrabbit investing," on the other hand, often zips here and there and never reaches the other side of the road. How soon you start socking away money each month and let compounding help you will determine your wealth. For a sure-fire saving strategy, start small, start now, stick to it, and let the magic of compounding do the job.

Whether you're in your forties or fifties, the principle remains the same. Let's say you can pay yourself first and save $200 a month. If you invest in an equity stock mutual fund, based on recent history, you'll earn a total return of about 15 percent a year. At the end of 20 years, with all dividends reinvested, your account should total about $283,000. If you invest that same $200 a month for only 15 years, you'll have only about $131,000 in the account, or less than half that amount.

Here's what the magic of compounding tells us:

- Lesson one: The additional five years, with only another $12,000 saved and invested between the 15th and 20th year, resulted in the return of an extra $140,000 ($152,000 less $12,000).
- Lesson two: Since you effectively earn interest on interest, you get a whopping $11,750 average annual return on your money for continuing to save and invest $2,400 each year for 20 years.

I know what you're thinking. You're as tense as a first-time bungee jumper, and you're staring at these numbers saying, "Now I know why people who save money over time become rich."

Compounding is boring. But if you give it time, it works. It's the secret of long-term financial success. Most people believe they won't save any money once they retire. In our example, if you can continue to save for an additional five years after you retire, you can build up your financial nest egg.

Here's another example.

Say you have a child or grandchild who has turned 18 years of age. You'd like to make him or her a millionaire by the age of 65, but you don't know how. What can you do? You can open an "early bird" individual retirement account for the young person. What you get once again is the awesome power of compounding over a period of time.

Assume the individual has at least $2,000 of earned income a year. You can then make a gift of $2,000 for him or her to put in an IRA. If you do this for eight years, or a total of $16,000, at the child's age 65, assuming an annual return of 10 percent, compound interest will have built the IRA to over a million dollars.

Let's say the individual waits only eight years, to age 27, to begin socking away the $2,000 a year in an IRA. Now he or she must contribute $2,000 for the next 39 years, until age 65. By waiting eight years to start making annual contributions, the return at age 65, after subtracting the original $78,000 investment, is only about $800,000. In other words, starting at age 27 the return is only 11-fold, while starting at age 19 the return is 64-fold.

If you've already reached mid-life, say age 35, does the time value of money work for you? Yes, it does. If you put $2,000 a year into an IRA for the next 30 years, using the same example, earning 10 percent a year, the $60,000 will grow to a whopping $361,000 at age 65.

If you are totally confused by all these examples of compounding, here's what I mean when I say it's never too late to get rich: You can become a millionaire by the time you're 65.

If you invest in good-performing stock mutual funds, leave the money in the fund and earn a 12 percent annual return (the Standard & Poor's 500 stock index of major corporations has returned each year, on average, 12 percent over the last 50 years), you'll reach the magic number without any further effort on your part. There is no guarantee that the stock market will repeat its last 50-year track record, but even a lower return could still grow substantially over time.

The following table shows the amount needed to earn $1 million at age 65, assuming a 12 percent annual return:

Age	One-Time Investment or Monthly Investments		Value at 65
20	$ 6,098	$ 59	$1,000,000
25	10,748	104	1,000,000
35	33,378	328	1,000,000
40	58,823	594	1,000,000
50	182,696	2,121	1,000,000

If these figures seem too daunting, there's no reason why you shouldn't do something less. If you were 40 years old, you could accumulate $250,000 by age 65 by investing $14,706, or $149 a month.

Does compounding work only when you invest money? No. The secret of building equity in your home is the reverse of earning income by saving on interest. Most lenders make it easy to send in extra money each month by checking the box for extra principal payments. You can do this on a regular basis or whenever you have the extra cash.

Before you dismiss this idea, consider what just a few pennies a day can do to cut your mortgage interest bill. Just 25 cents a day on an average 30-year fixed mortgage at 8 percent can save you over $7,000 in interest costs over the life of the loan. Author Marc Eisenson says, "Just imagine what you can do saving 50 cents a day and paying that on your mortgage. The average savings, over the term of the mortgage, is about $15,000. If you can save $1 a day, you'll save about $26,000." (*The Banker's Secret,* Box 78, Elizaville, NY 12523, 914-758-1400.)

You can also reduce your mortgage term by sending in extra monthly payments. Here are the extra amounts you'd need to pay each month to pay off a 30-year fixed-rate mortgage early:

To Pay Off a 30-Year Mortgage @ 7% in:

Loan Amount	25 Years	20 Years	15 Years
$ 75,000	$31.11	$ 82.50	$175.15
100,000	41.47	109.99	233.52
160,000	66.36	175.99	373.64
200,000	82.95	219.99	467.05

SOURCE: Marc Eisenson, *The Banker's Secret.*

Although you may not live in the home for 30 years, paying off your mortgage early will give you more equity when you are ready to buy another home. It's like making a down payment on your next home before you buy.

Basic Rule #4:

Continue to save each year.

Why is this rule important? In one word: inflation. As your income rises over the years, you can boost your annual savings and offset rising inflation by paying yourself first. *The only people who worry about inflation are those who don't pay themselves first.*

Money has value only for what it will buy when you spend it. I can remember the Great Depression, when inflation worked in reverse and prices fell. From that experience of being poor, I still pick up pennies from the street. I don't need the money, and today inflation has made the penny almost obsolete, but once you begin to save money "a penny saved is a penny earned."

By the 1950s and 1960s, inflation was running around 3 percent a year. It soared to about 10 percent a year in the early 1980s and then fell back to around 5 percent a year for the rest of the decade. In the future, inflation will be our economic "enemy number one." Remember your first monthly salary? Today, it might buy groceries. Callers to my radio show and subscribers to my newsletter tell me that by the time their kids go to college, the cost of a college education will be beyond their reach. For the last decade, the cost of a college education has been rising twice as fast as the rate of family income, but our savings rate has not kept up with inflation. Figure 1.1 illustrates how inflation has eroded our buying power in recent years.

Suppose you had saved $20,000 in 1972 toward your future retirement nest egg. Over the past two decades, inflation has eroded the purchasing power of $20,000 to about 40 percent of its original value. Looked at another way, $20,000 would have had to grow to about $50,000 just to keep pace with inflation.

This rule tells you to continue to save more each year as your salary increases over the years. Once you retire and the paycheck stops, you face the challenge of keeping up with inflation because

Figure 1.1   Decreasing Purchasing Power

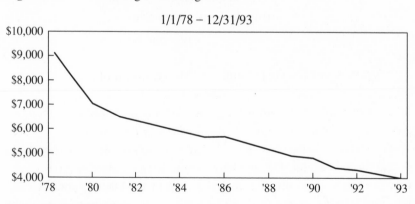

SOURCE: Consumer Price Index.

people today live longer. A 62-year-old retiree today is expected to live another 22 years. The earlier you plan to retire, the longer you're expected to live, and the longer your money may have to last. Since you'll have less time to let compounding work to meet your goal, figure on boosting your annual savings and investments by about 5 percent for each year you plan to retire before age 65.

Now you know how to overcome that paralyzing fear in the pit of your stomach that you're earning a reasonable paycheck each month, yet you can't build up a sizable nest egg to overcome future inflation, the skyrocketing cost of college and a retirement within your current standard of living. The good news is that you don't have to become a phenomenal stock picker or find a few lucky investments, but you do have to follow the time-honored rule of saving money first, allowing compounding to work for you and investing in conservative American stocks.

I said at the beginning of this chapter that using the magic of compound interest to gain wealth was simple, but boring. How easy is it? Suppose that at the start of 1981 you had invested $10,000 in a good growth stock fund. The fund had an annual total return, with dividends and capital gains reinvested at net asset value, equal to the overall stock market's recent average of about 15 percent a year. The awesome power of compounding would have turned the original $10,000 investment into about $61,500 by 1993—just 13 years later. The gain of $51,500 works out, on average, to be an annual return of $3,961 on the original $10,000 investment. Of course, this would have been possible only if you had stayed in the stock market at all times, burying your head in the sand like an ostrich.

Once you start investing in the stock market, look on the bright side. You don't need perfect timing or fabulous information, nor do you need to be let in on the ground floor. You only need to be invested—and stay invested—in good-performing stock mutual funds. If the market is up, you'll feel comfortable buying more mutual fund shares. If the market is flat, it's a chance to invest at today's prices. If the market is down, stocks are cheaper and you'll get more shares of the fund. The important point is to continue to save and invest each month no matter what's happening in the stock market.

Again, let me emphasize that the main reason people in America aren't prosperous today is that they didn't save part of their income first, and, once saved, they didn't invest and let the magic of compounding make them wealthy. Saving money can have a lasting effect. I remember how good I felt as a young person when my bank balance went up by even a quarter and how much it hurt when I had to withdraw the money.

The final payoff is this: If you save regularly, you'll feel like your life is under control and you can look to the future confident that you can meet unexpected emergencies and provide a decent life for yourself in retirement.

CHAPTER 2

Lender Beware

*I*ndividuals have loaned money in return for interest payments since money was invented. It was not until 1472, however, when what many consider to be the oldest bank in the world, the Monte Dei Paschi Di Siena in Italy, introduced the forerunner of the passbook savings account. The idea that banks could attract individual savings *and* keep track of their accounts opened the door to massive lending. In Renaissance times, bankers like the Medicis and the Fuggers, with their state-licensed money machine to attract depositors' money, grew wealthy.

Beyond the Passbook

The passbook savings account remained the principal mode of individual savings for almost 500 years, until the advent of computers after World War II. The first stage of the technological revolution was internal. Since banks and thrifts are nothing more than giant countinghouses, it was easy to run the entire customer list past the computer each day. Earned interest, which had been posted once a month or once a quarter, could now be posted every night. It was a small step, to be sure, but in the merchandising of money, it was a fundamental innovation.

In 1969, an enterprising young executive of the Worcester Five Cents Savings Bank petitioned the Massachusetts Banking Department for permission to offer a *negotiable order of withdrawal account*. A NOW account was, in effect, a computer-driven checking account that paid interest on the balance in the account. The executive knew he was skating on thin ice because at that time it was illegal for federally insured banks and savings and loans to pay interest on any monies on deposit for less than 30 days. However, the Massachusetts savings banks had their own deposit insurance fund, and Massachusetts law did not have the same tight restrictions as those that governed the federally insured banks and thrifts.

The state bank regulators gave his suggestion of using computers to track interest rates on checking accounts a frigid reception and turned him down cold, but the enterprising executive believed he had found a formula that could pry open the regulatory gate. He sued—and he won. Thereafter, it became possible for state-chartered savings and loans to offer checking accounts that paid interest. For the first time since the advent of banking in the late 1400s, banks faced competition for the "free" money their customers had been forced to keep in non-interest-bearing checking accounts. As a result of this determined banking executive, who used the new computers and marketing to attract new banking customers, Congress authorized NOW accounts for federally insured banks and savings and loans.

Just as scientists have a hard time predicting earthquakes, we can seldom predict exactly where and when new ideas will jolt our financial system, but once the quake begins, once a new idea gives consumers a better deal, the change can shake the foundations of our free enterprise business world and set in motion a reordering to conform to a new set of realities.

Today, we take for granted that computers make possible money market accounts, certificates of deposits, NOW checking accounts and an endless array of bond mutual funds. While rich rewards may await the nimble and courageous bond buyer, safe returns the bank saver and fabulous profits the stock buyer, there are only two ways to put your money to work: either as a lender or as an investor.

A Lender Be

When you deposit money in a savings account, you are a lender. You are "lending" money to, say, a bank, in exchange for interest income. A lender's first objective is to keep his or her money safe. The next objective is to earn interest income. Therefore, lenders are willing to accept lackluster returns of 4 percent or less for the assurance that their original investment will be returned intact. The only decision they have to make is the length of the deposit term and the interest rate they'll accept. After the Great Depression and scores of bank failures, many lenders felt they were walking on a financial high wire. To give them the safety they require, Uncle Sam, through the Federal Deposit Insurance Corporation (FDIC), provides protection up to $100,000 per account.

Banks and thrifts offer two basic instruments for earning interest income: money market accounts and fixed-term certificates of deposit.

Money Market Accounts

Think of a money market account as a computerized passbook savings account. In the banking trade, they are called *demand deposits*. As with passbook savings, the main attraction is that you can make deposits and withdrawals any time you like. For this privilege you earn about 1 or 2 percent less in interest than you would with a fixed-term deposit. At the same time, money market mutual funds, while they are not federally insured, have had the same safety record as bank and savings and loan money market accounts, and they pay as much as 1 percent more interest.

Is there any reason for investing in a money market account? Probably not. If you want liquidity, you can find it in a vast array of income funds with much higher yields. Are money market accounts and passbook savings good for the bank? You bet they are! Over the past two decades, the banking industry has been sustained by the profits from ultra-low-yielding savings accounts that worried or uninformed lenders kept squirreled away in the bank. The good news, not for the lenders but for the taxpayers, is that without these billions of dollars of low-interest money the recent financial bailout of banks and savings and loans would have cost a great deal more.

Fixed-Term Deposits

Insured certificates of deposit are *term deposits*. Terms are available from six months to as long as ten years. As with bonds, the longer the term, the higher the yield. Six-month insured CDs might yield 3 percent, but a five-year CD could yield well over 5 percent. To keep the money locked up inside the bank once you've made the deposit, the bank or savings and loan imposes a penalty for "early withdrawal." The penalty is the loss of interest income for various periods, from 90 days to six months.

The problem with an insured CD is that if interest rates later rise, you are stuck with the lower yields, just as you would be with a bond. In your search for higher yields, you must withdraw the CD money and possibly pay the hefty early withdrawal penalty. With a bond, you can sell the bond at a possible loss of market value. In either case, you are hurt by rising interest rates. When rates are expected to rise, your best bet is to lock up the money for shorter terms.

If you deposit $1,000 in a one-year insured certificate of deposit, you are assured of the return of the $1,000 one year later. A bank or savings and loan failure along the way is no problem. Your money is safe. Or is it?

Actually, the assured safe return of your money in the face of rising inflation puts your money at great risk. The shrinking dollar a lender gets back has less value—that is, purchasing power—than when it was invested in the first place. For example, if you earn the inflation rate in interest (and this is difficult to do on most bank and savings and loan fixed-term deposits), you can go directly to the poorhouse without passing go and the $100 payoff. Here's why:

Inflation Rate	After-Tax, After-Inflation Return	
	4%	*5%*
Investment	$10,000	$10,000
Interest income	400+	500+
Total, before tax	10,400	10,500
Less taxes @ 28%	112−	140−
After tax	10,288	10,360
Less inflation	411−	518−
Buying power at year-end	9,877	9,842

As you can see, if you are a lender and want to preserve the future purchasing power of your money, your first objective is to earn an interest rate higher than inflation and taxes just to break even. Can lenders break even with insured CDs? Not based on experience, which shows that most lenders' yields are below the inflation and income tax rates.

With insured CD rates near historical lows and millions of customers pouring money into mutual funds, what's a bank or savings and loan to do? Answer: offer a federally insured CD with mutual fund returns without mutual fund risks. It's like investing in the stock market with Uncle Sam guaranteeing that you won't lose a penny if the stock market takes a dive. The idea of these stock market-based CDs is to earn income based on the Standard & Poor's 500 stock index rather than interest income. The CDs take the average level of the S&P 500 during each of the 36 months (with a three-year CD) or 60 months (with a five-year CD) and pay interest equal to twice the average percentage increase. The CD will return a few percentage points lower than if you invested directly in the S&P 500 because of the lack of dividends and because the CD does not compound earnings.

First offered in 1987, stock market CDs are now sprouting up nationwide. As with stock mutual funds, no one knows what income you'll earn; that's based on the performance of the stock market, but the new CDs come with some hefty drawbacks.

While you have a higher interest income potential than you do with a traditional CD, the income is paid annually so you can't delay the payouts to take advantage of higher stock market returns in future years as you can with a mutual fund.

The early withdrawal penalty requires a withdrawal from principal, not loss of interest, as with most regular CDs. A typical three-year stock market CD might impose early withdrawal penalties of 20 percent of your investment in the first year, 15 percent in the second and 10 percent in the third. Some banks and savings and loans limit stock market CDs to retirement plans such as IRAs, Keogh plans and other retirement plans, while others offer them to their regular customers for personal investing.

Since stock market-insured CDs return less than an S&P 500 stock index mutual fund, what's the deal? For people who seek maximum safety, this loss of potential income is offset by federal deposit insurance in case the stock market takes a major dive when the CD matures.

Truth-in-Savings Act

For the first time, banks and savings and loans will have to tell you what you'll actually earn on a savings account and what strings come attached to the fancy offer in the newspaper or magazine. In the past, because of the fine print and fees, the saver could actually earn less than advertised.

All yields on savings accounts must be expressed in terms of *annual percentage yield,* or APY. For example, if you deposit $1,000 with an APY of 5 percent, your account at the end of the year will total $1,050. It sounds simple, but the fine print can still reduce your interest income if all you do is look for the highest APY.

Advertisements for savings accounts must list the APY and the strings attached, but they aren't required to list all the details. For example, say you pass up a bank offering only 3 percent APY with no fees and deposit your $1,000 in a bank offering an APY of 7 percent but with a hefty fee of $5 a month to maintain your deposit. In the first bank, you'd earn $30 at the end of the year; in the other bank, only $10, a 1 percent return ($70 earned interest, less $60 in fees). Also consider when and how often the bank credits interest to the account. The best is daily compounding, and the worst is no compounding at all, called *simple interest.*

Before you make a deposit at a bank or savings and loan, ask for an account disclosure booklet, which lists all the fees, compounding and restrictions.

Basic Rule #5:

Lenders always take a risk.

There is no way you can put your money to work without some risk. You can play it safe with a federally insured savings account and risk rising inflation and low yields, or you can reach out for higher yields with bonds and risk the possible loss of your principal. If you've ever wondered why some people earn 3 percent while others earn 7 percent on bonds, it's because the higher yields carry greater risks to principal if interest rates later rise. If this sounds a bit cold-blooded, you're right.

Bond Basis Risk

Today, savvy lenders, dissatisfied with the skimpy yields on money market accounts and certificates of deposit, have discovered that they can double their interest income with bond mutual funds. Before you lend your money to a bank, a savings and loan or a bond mutual fund, you should understand bond basis risk. This knowledge of how changes in interest rates affect principal is the key to boosting your yields above the inflation rate. If you invest in longer-term bonds or bond funds without this knowledge, you can get clobbered if interest rates later rise.

Bond basis risk means that bond prices and yields move in opposite directions. Take a recent newspaper story on the bond market. "Treasury bond prices posted sharp gains today with the price of 30-year Treasury bonds rising 25/32 point, or $7.81 per $1,000 face value, while its yield fell from 6.30 percent to 6.24 percent."

Here's how bond basis risk can affect your original investment. Suppose that two years ago you purchased a $1,000 bond paying 7 percent. Now, two years later, you decide to sell your investment, but the current interest rate is 8 percent. You call your broker and find that your $1,000 bond is now worth only about $945. You are told that you have a *discounted bond*. Anyone who buys your bond, which is paying only 7 percent when current interest rates are 8 percent, will receive a discount so that the new investment will effectively earn 8 percent.

On the other hand, if interest rates have fallen to 6 percent after two years and you decide to sell your bond, you may be offered $1,055. You now have a *premium bond,* and a new buyer will pay the higher price to earn the bond's 7 percent yield when current rates are only 6 percent.

The degree of risk in bonds depends on how much interest rates move up or down and on the maturity of the bond. The longer the maturity, the greater the risk of loss or gain. For example, a money market account has no bond basis risk because the short maturities, often only 60 to 90 days, do not affect the price. A dollar invested in a money market fund will always be worth a dollar, but a dollar invested in a five-year bond when interest rates rise one full percentage point can clip the value of your investment by about 4 percent. That same one percentage point rate increase in a 30-year bond, however, can reduce the market value of your bond by more than 11 percent.

The following table shows how the market value of a $1,000 fixed-income investment can change if interest rates rise or fall one percentage point:

Investment	*Yield*	*1% Rise*	*1% Fall*
Money market	2.75%	-0-	-0-
5-year bond	6%	−$41	+$43
30-year bond	7.5%	−$110	+$133

Since longer-term bonds provide higher yields, and higher yields make selling income mutual funds easier, the chances are that, if you're earning high yields today, you're in a long-term bond fund.

High yields, however, are not the only factor to consider. Total return, which includes both bond price and yield, is a better measure of your investment's value. Total return is what you will earn at the end of the year, and it should include your interest income plus or minus any changes in the market value of the bonds and minus any sales charges and annual management fees.

The table below estimates total return on Treasury notes and bonds with varying maturities. As you can see, the longer the maturity, the greater the fluctuation in total return.

	Interest Rate	*Rates Remain Unchanged*	*Rates Go Up 1%*	*Rates Go Down 1%*
Short-term bond (3 years)	4.5%	+4.6%	+2.7%	+6.5%
Intermediate-term bond (10 years)	6%	+6.1%	−0.6%	+13.4%
Long-term bond (30 years)	7%	+7.1%	−4.3%	+21.0%

The column group heading "*Changes in Total Return*" spans the last three columns (*Rates Remain Unchanged*, *Rates Go Up 1%*, *Rates Go Down 1%*).

SOURCE: *Fidelity Focus*, Published by Fidelity Investments. Copyright 1993 FMR Corp. Reprinted with permission.

For example, on a $1,000 30-year bond, if rates rise one full percentage point your total return, including the 7 percent interest rate you earn, less the reduced market value should you sell, can be a loss of $43.

On the other hand, if rates fall one full percentage point, you can make a lot of money investing in long-term bonds. Should you sell a year later, based on this example, your total return, with interest earned and capital gains, would be a whopping profit of $210, or over 20 percent.

Basic Rule #6:

Don't buy bonds based solely on yield.

While you may shop for an insured certificate of deposit on yield, don't shop for fixed-income bonds or bond funds the same way. Remember, you're entering the land of the unpredictable, where half of Wall Street is looking to boost the value of your investment, and the other half is looking for fire-sale prices. Also, don't ever come into the bond market with the idea that you've got it all figured out. You can cut your losses and boost your profit by understanding the degree of risk you take *before* you invest.

Money mangers say it's best to invest with maturities of about three to five years. Five years is where the yield curve tends to flatten out; after that, you run more risk than reward by grabbing the higher yields. It's important to understand that bond basis risk holds true for *any* bond—government, tax-exempt municipal, high-yield junk or blue-chip corporate bonds.

Basic Rule #7:

When interest rates rise, the market value of your bond declines; when rates fall, the value increases.

How Safe Is "Safe"?

The major problem that bond investors encounter is that they don't fully understand the words "guarantee" and "safety" as applied to bonds. The guarantee stems from the fact that the bonds are unlikely to default. When you are told that a bond investment is "completely safe," it means simply that the bond issuer can be depended upon to pay the full face value of the bond at the end of the particular term. "Guarantee" and "safety" say nothing about bond basis risk—the risk that the value of the bond will be adversely affected by rising interest rates.

I can't tell you how many times readers of my newspaper column or listeners to my radio show ask me why, if they invested in safe, guaranteed bond investments, are they are losing money? A typical on-the-air conversation goes like this:

"Now listen, Mr. Jorgensen, I invested in this bond fund because the broker told me it was safe. They are government-backed bonds, and they were guaranteed. Now look here, the value of my original $50,000 investment is now worth only $44,000, and I can't afford to lose a penny."

"Did your broker explain bond basis risk?" I asked.

"What do you mean?"

"Let me put it this way. Since interest rates have risen since you invested in your bonds, the market value has declined big time. You may have been attracted by the very high yields you could earn, but you assumed big risks to get that high return."

"All he ever said was that I could earn high returns on guaranteed government-backed bonds. I'll kill him."

Insured Certificates of Deposit

Most people who invest in insured CDs believe that they are doing so without risk, but CDs, like bond income funds, also have drawbacks.

- The shorter the term, the lower the interest rate. This is the same for bond funds. For example, interest rates might be 3.95 percent for an 18-month CD but only 3.20 percent for a six-month CD. That's a 19 percent cut in rates to go shorter term. In effect, you are paying for the bond basis risk in advance by taking a lower interest rate. In a bond fund, should you sell, you'd take a loss only if rates rise, but you'd realize a profit if rates fell.

- You pay a penalty for early withdrawal. On six-month and nine-month CDs, the loss might be three months' worth of interest. On CDs over one year, the loss could be six months of interest. If your account has not earned enough interest income when you make the withdrawal, the bank can dip into your principal to make up the difference. With bond income funds, you have no early withdrawal penalty; any part of the money is quickly available without charge.

Where Lenders Can Invest Today

One of the best places to earn interest income today is by lending money to the state and federal government. Drowning in budgets of red ink, they offer investments with high returns and about the same safety as an insured savings account. Banks, of course, know this. Their job obligates them to search out the best return on their deposits, commensurate to the risk. What do banks and savings and loans do? While they pay lenders 3 percent on consumer savings, the savvy bank money managers take the deposits directly to the government and double their yields by investing in U.S. Treasury securities. In fact, the nation's banks now own more government debt than they have loans outstanding to businesses. With this spread—the difference between what a bank pays for money and what it earns—at record highs, any attempt to pry consumers away from ultra-low-yielding savings accounts is bad for business. As a result, for 1992 and 1993, many banks reported record profits.

As usual, it seems that the suits on Wall Street know more about banks than do consumers. In 1993, while most consumers were earning around 3 percent on their savings account money, those who invested in the top five mutual funds that invested only in bank and savings and loan stock earned a total return of about five times that of an insured CD. If all that sounds a bit crazy, you're right. The no-risk protection of FDIC insurance costs the investor a sizable loss on every $100 invested.

Basic Rule #8:

Smart lenders do their own homework.

Most lenders put their money to work by walking into a bank or savings and loan office, opening an account, filling out the paperwork, writing a check and taking what interest income they can get. It's easy. The financial institution does all the investing for you. But these turbulent times aren't for the meek who follow in the footsteps of the past. If you want to earn a decent return on the money you lend, you need to manage your money actively. Increasingly, savvy lenders are seeking out the best yields, filling out the paperwork themselves and sending in their check at a total cost of 29 cents. The startling news is that do-it-yourself lenders can double their interest rate returns with essentially the same safety as a low-yielding bank account.

Think in terms of objectives. If you want to earn interest income, the important points are yield and safety. Here are just four possible alternatives to insured savings accounts:

Series EE Savings Bonds

In 1993, the U.S. Treasury Department lowered the guaranteed rate on savings bonds from 6 percent to 4 percent. Since savings bonds aren't for long-term savings, this opened up an opportunity for lenders to boost their short-term yields over insured CDs. That's because you can hold EE savings bonds for a minimum of six months, and with current guaranteed rates of 4 percent, the yield can top many bank or savings and loan yields for the same term by as much as 1 percent. Banks and thrifts are unhappy over the government's competition for their business of attracting deposits, so to prevent a run on ultra-low-yielding savings accounts at the bank, the government limits the purchase of Series EE bonds to $30,000 face value ($15,000 issue price) per person per year.

100% Treasury Securities Mutual Funds

Another idea for lenders is a 100 percent Treasury fund, which comes with two options. For very safe lending, the short-term funds (two- to four-year maturities) yield about 2 percent more than the average CD, and the intermediate-term funds (five- to eight-year maturities) yield almost double the average bank return. Because these funds are invested 100 percent in U.S. Treasury securities, the income is exempt from state and local income taxes. Many of the no-load funds come with the options of reinvesting your money or making withdrawals by check as you need the money.

Short-Duration Government Funds

These funds limit the average maturity of their portfolios to three-year Treasury notes. These shorter maturities limit the bond basis risk. For example, if short-term rates rise by 100 basis points (1 percent), the fund expects the market value of the fund to decline by approximately 1.9 percent. If the net asset value of one share of the fund is $10.00, the value of a share would then only fall to about $9.81.

What this all means is that the difference between taking no investment risk and just a little bit of risk is substantial in terms of return. The reward for this tiny risk? With one-year insured certificates of deposit yielding around 3 percent, the short-duration funds were yielding around 6 percent. If short-term interest rates rose by a full percentage point, your $1,000 account would look like this:

Earned interest @ 6%	$ 60
Less 1.9% loss of principal	−19
Total return year-end	$ 41

If you sell at the end of the year, that's a return of 4.1 percent, substantially more than the 3 percent return on the fixed savings account.

Municipal Bonds

And now, as they say on Monty Python, for "something completely different"—earning interest income *without* paying taxes. The best opportunities for hefty yields in recent years have been municipal bonds. States, cities, towns, water districts, school districts, highways and even the local hospital all need to borrow money. And when they do, they offer lenders interest income that is free of most income taxes. But not all income is tax-free. If the fund pays out realized capital gains, those payouts are fully taxable. These dividends are, in effect, a profit accumulated on the increased value of the bonds inside the fund.

Municipal bonds—"munis"—come in several different forms, depending on the risk of interest payments and the repayment of the bond. There are two major types of municipal bonds. General obligation bonds (GOs) are the safest tax-free bonds you can buy because the payments for interest and principal come from general tax revenues. Agencies that issue GOs can raise taxes, if necessary, to pay bondholders. Revenue bonds (REVs) are issued for a specific project such as construction of a bridge, a power plant, a hospital or housing project. The income to pay the bondholders is expected to come from the revenues generated by the specific project. The risk is that if the income from the project fails to generate enough money to pay interest or pay off the bonds, the bonds can default. Although this is rare, defaults do happen. About ten years ago, the Washington Public Power Supply System, which became known as "WOOPS," defaulted on $2.25 billion of revenue bonds because the nuclear power plants they financed, which were to generate electric power, were never built. This was the largest default in history, and it told investors that one of the risks in revenue bonds is political risk.

Municipal bonds are also issued as bond anticipation notes (BANs), which are short-term notes with repayment from the proceeds of an upcoming bond issue yet to be sold, and tax anticipation notes (TANs), which are short-term notes similar to BANs, with repayment from expected tax revenue. There are other types of municipal bonds, but for most investors these are the most important.

For lenders who want an extra degree of safety, municipal bond insurance is available. It is underwritten by private insurers and guarantees both the timely payment of interest and the repayment of the bonds at maturity. Most of the bond insurance is written by two organizations: American Municipal Bond Assurance Corporation (AMBAC) and Municipal Bond Insurance Association (MBIA).

How To Compute Equivalent Yields

With municipal bond investing it helps to understand tax equivalent yields. Let me put it this way: If you're earning around

4 percent fully taxable at the bank or thrift and are in a combined federal tax bracket of 28 percent, your net income after taxes is only 2.88 percent. Municipal bond funds, during this same period, paid around 5 percent tax-free.

To see how illogical this whole idea of earning interest income has become, consider this: As I write this book, the national average annualized percentage yield for a bank money market account, according to *Bank Rate Monitor*, is 2.31 percent. The annualized percentage yield for a tax-free money market account is 2.42 percent. That's right. You can earn more interest income by *not* paying taxes! Millions of people, afraid to leave the safety of a bank or savings and loan, and in a 28 percent federal bracket, are netting, in this example, 1.80 percent on their savings, while the savvy lender with a tax-free money market fund is earning 2.42 percent.

To calculate the value of your current taxable yield compared to a muni's yield, take your current tax rate, written as a decimal, and subtract it from 1.00. If your marginal tax rate is 28 percent, subtract .28 from 1.00 and get .72. If the tax-free bond fund is yielding 5 percent, divide 5 by .72 and get 6.94 percent, the tax equivalent yield you need to equal the municipal bond's yield of 5 percent.

If you live in a state like California, with hefty state income taxes rates, your combined tax rate might be 37 percent (28 percent federal and 9 percent state). Your calculations would be 1.00 minus .37, or .63. Divide the 5 percent tax-free yield by .63 and you see that you need to earn a taxable yield of 7.93 percent to match the 5 percent tax-free yield.

If you live in a state with state income taxes, it's important to consider double tax-free municipal bond funds. These so-called "single-state" mutual funds invest in bonds issued in your state, so the income generally qualifies for both federal and state tax exemption. If you live in a state without state income taxes, you can shop for nationwide municipal bond funds. Here's a table to help you check what tax-free yields are worth. It does not take into account state and local income taxes, if any.

	A Tax-Free Yield of:					
	4.0%	4.5%	5.0%	5.5%	6.0%	6.5%
Tax Bracket	*Is Equivalent to a Taxable Yield of:*					
0 %	4.0	4.5	5.0	5.5	6.0	6.5
15 %	4.7	5.3	5.9	6.5	7.0	7.6
28 %	5.5	6.2	6.9	7.6	8.3	9.0
31 %	5.8	6.5	7.2	8.0	8.7	9.4
36 %	6.2	7.0	7.8	8.6	9.4	11.0
39.6%	6.6	7.4	8.3	9.1	10.7	11.6

As you can see, earning interest income has become so goofy that even if you're in a zero tax bracket, you'll still do better with tax-free bonds.

Basic Rule #9:

Smart investors keep maturities short.

Again, let me say that millions of fixed-income investors will lose money in the years to come because they don't understand the risk they are taking on so-called "safe" and "guaranteed" long-term bonds or bond funds. They look at the hefty yield, listen to the soothing talk from the broker or financial planner on how much better they can do with their money, grab the deal, and then lose their shirts.

How ridiculous can this whole episode of investing long term become? Consider the new "Mickey Mouse" bonds issued by the Walt Disney Company. For the first time since 1954, a borrower has offered 100-year bonds. Yielding barely one percentage point more than a 30-year bond, the market value of these bonds, with a maturity in 2093, will fall like a rock when interest rates rise.

Zero Coupon Bonds

Zero coupon bonds get their name from the fact that bond certificates once came with interest coupons attached to the bond for interest payment. These were *bearer bonds*, so called because they were considered the property of anyone who held them. Zero coupon bonds, on the other hand, don't pay interest each year, so they, in effect, have no coupons. Zero coupon bonds are sold at a discount from face value and return to the investor the full amount of the bond at maturity. They work just like U.S. savings bonds that cost $25 and return $50 at maturity. You can buy zeros for almost any length of time. For a long-term zero (about 20 years), you might pay just $250 for a $1,000 bond; for shorter maturities (about 5 years), you might pay $750 for the same bond.

But zeros do earn interest income—the difference between the purchase price and face of the bond—and this interest is treated by the Internal Revenue Service as ordinary income in the year it is credited to your account. Many people don't like paying taxes on interest income they don't receive each year, so brokers suggest you put the zeros in your IRA or other retirement plans where taxes are delayed until you take out the money.

Zero coupon bonds are sold as a "hands-off" investment, and they are. You can buy a 15-year zero bond, put it in a safe deposit box, and collect the full face value of the bond 15 years later. What you are gambling on is that during this period interest rates won't change because zero coupon bonds are about three times more volatile in price than traditional bonds. With long-term zero coupon bond mutual funds, the share price can skyrocket with falling rates; with rising interest rates, the share price can plunge, making many people feel like they're sitting in a deck chair on the Titanic.

Why do people buy zero coupon bonds? Because they sound so simple, because they can fill a need—like saving for college expenses 16 years from today—and because they are very profitable for brokers and financial planners to sell. Once again, the suits who run around Wall Street have been able to fashion zero coupon bonds from a wide array of bonds. There are tax-free zeros, corporate zeros and Treasury zeros (sometimes known as TIGRs, CATS and STRIPS). The banks, not to be left out, offer federally insured zero certificates of deposit.

Ginnie Mae Bonds

With bank interest rates depressed to pathetically low rates, many individual investors have turned to mortgage-backed securities as a way to boost yields. The most popular investment is Ginnie Mae bond funds. Ginnie Mae bonds are named after the government agency that issues them, the Government National Mortgage Association (GNMA).

Here's how Ginnie Maes are created: A homeowner obtains a mortgage to buy a new home. The mortgage lender then sells the mortgage to GNMA to obtain money to make more loans. GNMA packages the loans and sells them to security firms who offer them in the form of a mutual fund.

Ginnie Maes work differently from all other bonds. The big difference is that, as homeowners repay their mortgages each month, the investor receives both a return of principal and interest income. Consequently, if you hold a Ginnie Mae bond to maturity, you'll end up with zero value. With regular bonds, your principal is repaid at maturity, when you sell or when the bond is called. With a Ginnie Mae mutual fund you can automatically reinvest both the return of principal and interest income, receive both in cash or a combination of each.

Ginnie Mae bond funds are often sold on the basis that they are safe from default by a government agency. That is true, but they are not safe from bond basis risk that can change the market value of the fund's share price at any time. Although Ginnie Maes have current yields almost three percentage points above most insured CDs, there is a danger for the investor if interest rates change. For every 1 percent rise or fall in interest rates, the market value of an average Ginnie Mae fund can change 6 percent. On rising rates, the bond fund can fall 6 percent in price; on falling interest rates, it can rise 6 percent in price. Also, Ginnie Mae funds are made up of mortgages with relatively high interest rates, and if rates fall, mortgages may be refinanced early, lowering the fund's yield. If interest rates rise, homeowners won't refinance, and yields may tend to lag the market. If you are thinking about investing in Ginnie Maes because of their current yield, you should also think about total return and carefully consider the volatility of the share price.

Collateralized Mortgage Obligations

Collateralized mortgage obligations (CMOs) are bonds composed of mortgages guaranteed by GNMA and FNMA (Fannie Mae, the Federal National Mortgage Association). CMOs were brought to market to offer investors various maturities, so each bond is divided into different classes, or tranches, with maturity dates from 3 years to 20 years. Although CMOs are safe from default, they are highly volatile in market price, and the possibility of losing money in some of them is great.

Shopping for a Bond Fund

Cutting through the confusion about yield and bond risk is not easy. Mutual funds like to tout the best numbers they can find, and when they've earned hefty returns in the past, they are eager to put these numbers in the headlines of their advertisements. Here's a checklist to help you get through the minefield of buzz words:

SEC Yield

This is the Securities and Exchange Commission's required way to state the so-called 30-day yield, minus fund expenses. It starts with the fund's income per share over the preceding 30 days, minus expenses, and adjusts for the market value of the bonds in the portfolio and other income. The results are divided by the fund's share price and annualized. It is the most reliable comparison between funds, but you'll earn this 30-day yield only if you stay invested in the bond for a year, if you make no dividend withdrawals and if the fund keeps paying at its recent rate.

12-Month Average Yield

This represents the fund's per share income during the past 12 months divided by the share price adjusted for capital gains. It only tells what you could have earned during the past year. If the hefty 12-month yield in the ad looks like it could pay for a spending spree through Monte Carlo, don't bank on it. Past returns are no guarantee of future payouts after you invest.

Total Return

Total return can be the most misleading number of all. It's figured by assuming that all dividends during the period are reinvested, that the fund's sales commissions are subtracted and that all capital gains or losses are included. If interest rates have fallen in the past year or years, the bond fund's total return will be displayed in big letters in the ad. That's because falling interest rates, as we've already learned, can boost capital gains and total returns. And the total return shown in the ad is not "spendable money" because it includes capital gains that are not realized until you sell the bond fund.

What all these numbers can mean to a new investor is best described by a recent newspaper advertisement for a bond fund offered by a savings and loan. It boasted a current yield of 6.6 percent when most savings deposits were paying around 3 percent. The fund sounded a lot better than an insured CD. In even bigger print, the ad told the would-be investor that the average total return for the most recent year was 7.53 percent, and over five years a hefty 8.98 percent.

But, as usual, the fine print told a different story. The years used to compute total return were a period when interest rates in general were falling, increasing capital gains profits substantially. Also, the bond fund had a 4 percent front-end sales commission, so investors in the first year could end up with lower returns than the low-yielding savings and loan CD they were leaving. What's more, if rates were to rise during the following year on these longer-term bond funds, the actual return could be much less than might be expected from the flashy ad.

For example, a $10,000 investment at 6.6 percent at year's end should have earned $660 in interest and be worth $10,660. However, with an up-front sales commission of 4 percent, the actual net investment would be only $9,600. At year's end, with interest income on that lower amount, the total would be only $10,233. That means it would have cost you $427 to let the savings and loan help you invest your money. Or, to put it another way, that's a 2.33 percent return on your original investment, not the hefty 6.6 percent highlighted in the ads.

But it gets worse. If rates rise one percentage point during the year, the total return can actually decline. That's because the market value of the bond fund could fall $50 per $1,000 of face value. In this example, on the $10,000 initial investment, the year-end total return could actually be:

- interest income of $633
- a capital loss $500
- a market value of $9,733

Should you sell after one year under this example, you'd take a loss of $267 on your original $10,000 investment.

Here's another example. With one-year CDs yielding 3 percent, a brokerage firm's ad for a long-term bond fund had big headlines that screamed:

Government Income Portfolio
8.00%

* Invests primarily in U.S. government securities
* Carries an AA rating by Standard & Poor's
* Pays quarterly dividends
* Trades on the New York Stock Exchange

Past performance does not guarantee future results. The distribution rate quoted above is the annualized monthly dividend divided by current market price as of 8/9/93. Return may fluctuate as will market price. Upon redemption, your investment may be worth more or less than you originally paid.

Let's look at the advertisement's key points and see what they mean:

- The fund says it invests "primarily" in U.S. government securities. What this tells you is that the fund may invest in a variety of government bonds, government-backed bonds and other high-quality bonds.
- The fund carries an AA rating from Standard & Poor's. S&P's top rating for bonds is AAA, followed by AA+, and then AA.
- The fund pays a quarterly dividend. True, but if you need more money from time to time, can you make withdrawals? You can't. To make withdrawals from the fund you must sell some shares and pay hefty brokerage fees.
- Since the fund is traded on the New York Stock Exchange, it is *closed-end*, and its shares trade like IBM, Ford or any other share of stock.
- The fine print tells you that the value of your investment can change daily. Therefore, the investment may be worth more (if rates decline) or less (if rates rise), and the stated 8 percent return may fluctuate in the future.

With a strongbox filled with this bond fund, you'll feel like you're riding shotgun on a stagecoach going backwards.

The lesson of this chapter is that many lenders, in their manic search for higher yields, are taking unusually high risks in the face of what most people believe will be a period of rising interest rates and lower bond prices during the next few years. Before you lend your hard-earned money, be sure you understand the basics of bond basis risk, total return and tax-free versus taxable. Then read all the fine print and make sure you know what it means.

CHAPTER 3

Investor Pitfalls

"Safety," the letter began. "Safety, safety, safety, but I want to earn more money than my CD pays. The broker is telling me I can double or triple my return with his mutual funds. Sounds like a good deal. What do you think?"

This letter is typical of the kind I receive from people who are about to leave the safety of bank savings and strike out for higher returns. In the past, they let the bank invest their money without apparent risk, and they have a pretty clear idea of how that works, but now they are bowing to the pressure of low yields and searching for something better.

The basic rule is that if you are not a lender, then you must be an investor. Unlike a lender, whose first priority is the safe return of his or her money, an investor knowingly takes a risk of loss. The risk is the possibility that an investment will not perform as expected. This tolerance for risk varies among individual investors, and you need to assess your own risk tolerance in order to avoid making panic decisions if your investment flames out.

If you invest in the stock market through a broker or financial planner, understand that you are on your own. Gary Wollin of Wedbush Morgan Securities in San Francisco, a broker with over 30 years on Wall Street, offers these four rules for losing the most money in the stock market in the shortest amount of time.*

- Buy whatever the telephone call is about. You'll probably talk to a broker who will fill your ear with his or her past conquests. You'll get calls for oil and gas wells, coins, Scotch, wine and every other hot idea under the sun. These people will help you invest your money until it's all gone. If you give your money to a stranger on the telephone, your chances of losing it are very great. Or, as Al Capone once said, "Anyone found sleeping in the trunk of a car deserves to be shot."

- Never, but never, take a loss. This rule, at first, may seem like nonsense. How can I lose a great deal of money if I never take a loss? It's simple. Buy a stock at $40 and hold on to it as it declines. Now it's selling at $12. "Well," you say, "if I haven't sold it, I really haven't lost anything." The problem is that the stock probably won't get back to what you paid for it. One of the secrets in investing in stocks is to know when to cut your losses. If you expect to always make a profit in the stock market, you're in for disappointment.

- Follow the stock tips. Brokers are in business to give you stock tips. So are your friends. Often a person buys 1,000 shares of a $50 stock because some stranger he met on a golf course told him that the stock was sure to go up. The basic fact is that no one knows for sure when a stock will go up. Often, by the time you buy the "hot" stock, it's already on its way down in price.

- Try to become rich fast. Lack of patience is probably the biggest single impediment to success in the stock market. With Wall Street and the media focusing on the big winners, most investors get the unrealistic expectation that they can win right away, and win big every time. Investing in the stock market is a long-term (over five years) project. The correct approach is to have the patience to get rich slowly.

---

*Reprinted by permission of Gary A. Wollin.

Many investors lose money investing in individual stocks or securities because they are not skilled in market timing and stock selection and they don't take the time to actively monitor their investments. Today, more and more people are getting around these problems by investing in stock mutual funds. A mutual fund is an organization that pools the money from thousands of investors, hires knowledgeable portfolio managers and invests in hundreds of companies in specific industries.

In only five years, the number of mutual funds has increased from about 2,400 to over 4,300—more than all the individual companies listed on the New York and American stock exchanges combined. In fact, the time is fast approaching when Americans will have more of their money invested in mutual funds than in banks. By the end of 1993, the total assets invested in mutual funds were estimated to pass $2 trillion. According to the Federal Reserve Board, slightly more than $2 trillion is now in all forms of savings accounts in the banking system.

The Investment Company Institute, the mutual fund trade group, reports that as of October 1993, assets were nearly evenly divided among stock funds ($620 billion), bond funds ($725 billion) and money market mutual funds ($559 billion). In 1992, 27 percent of U.S. households owned mutual funds, up from only 6 percent in 1980. The ownership of mutual funds across income categories of households varies very little. Eighteen percent of households owning mutual funds have incomes of less than $30,000; 28 percent have incomes from $30,000 to $49,999; 29 percent have incomes from $50,000 to $74,999; and 25 percent have incomes above $75,000.

When you invest in a stock mutual fund, you are investing in common stocks. A share of stock represents the ownership in a company. As a part owner, you share in the company's profits in the form of dividends as well as any increase in the price of the stock if the company grows and becomes more profitable. The risk is that the company could experience hard times and show a loss. In that case, the dividends could be cut or eliminated, the price of the stock could decline, or the company could even go out of business and the stock could become worthless.

The risk of investing in a mutual fund with a huge portfolio of stocks is a great deal less than the risk of purchasing individual common stocks. In fact, if the stock equity mutual fund's annual returns are no better than the overall stock market, then over time the risk is very slim indeed. For the past 66 years, from 1926 through 1992, the average annual return for common stocks was 10.4 percent. Over that same 66 years, long-term bonds returned 5.5 percent and Treasury bills just 3.75 percent. Over a ten-year period, from 1982 to 1991, the Standard & Poor's 500 stock index had an annual total return of 17.6 percent for investors, but the return on 30-day Treasury bills was only 7.7 percent.

The important point here is that you can find stock mutual funds with better-than-average performance to let you do even better. For example, for the period ending October 1, 1993, a major stock fund had an annualized total return, with dividends reinvested, of 26 percent for 3 years, 28 percent for 5 years, 15.4 percent for 10 years and 16.4 percent for 15 years.

Although the subject of making money in the stock market may seem like a bowl of spaghetti in mid-explosion, it's really not that complicated.

Basic Rule #10:

Learn the types of mutual funds.

Open-End Funds

Most people are familiar with open-end mutual funds that can be purchased from brokers, financial planners or directly from the mutual fund itself. They are called open-end because investors can redeem shares directly from the fund at any time at their current net asset value. Since there is no limit to the number of outstanding shares, a single open-end fund can hold billions of investment dollars.

The managers of open-end funds continually buy and sell securities that make up the fund as they see opportunities in the marketplace. This ability to buy and sell securities allows the portfolio fund managers to adjust to changing market conditions. As a result, open-end funds are often referred to as *managed funds*.

Closed-End Funds

Closed-end fund shares are traded on the stock exchanges, much like shares of Ford, IBM, General Electric and other corporations. The investor buys closed-end fund shares through a broker rather than through the fund itself. These funds have a limited number of shares outstanding, usually from an initial public offering (IPO), and the fund pools its money to buy bonds or stocks. The selling price of the shares may be above or below its net asset value. Above it, the shares sell at a premium; below it, they sell at a discount. That's because the price per share on the exchange is whatever a new investor will pay. Investing in a closed-end fund is much like buying common stock. You expect to make money on dividends, and you hope that the share price will rise after you buy so that you can realize a profit when you sell.

Why don't you hear more about closed-end funds? Open-end mutual fund managers spend a lot of money on advertising to attract new shareholders. That's because the more money they take in, the more shares they can issue, which in turn generates additional management fees and income. Since closed-end funds are limited in the number of new shares they can issue, there is no incentive to advertise. You usually hear about closed-end funds from a stockbroker or financial planner seeking to sell you these securities.

Comparison of Open-End and Closed-End Funds

Closed-end funds tend to be stable investments because they keep the same type of investment as listed in their IPO. Open-end funds have a freer hand and a wider choice of investments. Because closed-end funds don't issue new shares or need to buy back shares from shareholders, the fund managers can take the longer-term view and stay fully invested.

Open-end funds, on the other hand, must keep between 5 and 10 percent of their funds in cash to meet redemption demands, which often occur at the worst possible time for the fund, when the market is in a decline. Consequently, a significant part of your investment in open-end stock or bond funds is not invested in the securities, but is held as cash to redeem shares.

Interval Funds

To overcome this problem of having to hold huge amounts of cash for redemption requests, many open-end funds are expected to offer a new array of mutual funds that restrict investors' ability to redeem shares. The interval funds would limit withdrawals to specific times—to one day each quarter, for example—and investors who intended to sell their shares would have to notify the fund manager a month in advance.

Unit Investment Trusts

Another type of pooled investment is a unit investment trust that purchases securities such as corporate, municipal and government bonds or preferred stock. Unlike an open-end mutual fund, which constantly buys and sells securities, a unit trust purchases fixed portfolios of selected bonds and stocks. The income from a unit trust is more certain than that of a regular mutual fund, but, as with an individual security, interest rates or market conditions can change the market value of the trust.

At the end of 1992, the Investment Company Institute reported that there were a total of 12,623 tax-free bond trusts with a market value of $81 billion, 745 taxable bond trusts with a market value of $10 billion and 230 equity unit trusts with a market value of $6.5 billion.

Basic Rule #11:

**Learn which family of funds best
suits your needs *before* you invest.**

Most investors can limit their investment portfolios to just seven types of investments.

Interest Income Accounts and Funds

Income plans include bank savings accounts, money market accounts, money market funds and bond funds. These types of plans are best used for short-term savings with quick access to your money.

Money market mutual funds, both taxable and tax-free, are not insured, but they have never lost a penny of investors' money. They also maintain the market value of your investment by investing in short-term maturities of 60 to 90 days, so the share price is always $1.

Bond funds carry more risk, depending on the maturity of the portfolio. Short-term bond funds (3 to 6 years) offer the greatest safety, and they can be used for savings plans. On the other hand, long-term bond funds (20 to 30 years) are investments rather than savings accounts. They offer the highest yields, but also the greatest risk of principal.

General characteristics of all three types of short-term investments are current income with safety of principal and little potential capital growth.

Balanced Funds

This type of fund takes its name from the fact that the fund invests in both common stocks and bonds. The fund is balanced in whatever the portfolio manager believes is the best combination of stocks, bonds and cash. A typical balanced fund might have its portfolio invested 60 percent in common stocks, 30 percent in bonds and 10 percent in cash and preferred stock. Balanced funds usually have the least price volatility and the lowest return. For the stability of a steady share price, you often give up the chance of making big gains when the prices of higher-risk stocks soar.

General characteristics are moderate potential for capital growth, high to moderate current income and moderate stability of principal.

Asset Allocation Funds

These funds play the entire field, buying and selling stocks and bonds and holding cash in any combination. The selling points are diversity of investments and the flexibility to quickly respond to changing market conditions. An asset allocation fund might hold as much as 18 percent of its assets in short-term money market accounts and 30 percent in bonds if the fund manager thinks the market is about to decline.

The problem with asset allocation funds is that your results depend upon the fund manager's skill in outguessing the market, yet many managers fly by the seat of their pants in deciding when to buy and sell, whether or not to stay in the market and when to hold cash. These funds are, in effect, market-timing funds. The portfolio managers think they know when to buy and sell a security for maximum gain. A study of market timing, however, has concluded that an investment manager would have to be right on his or her market forecast 75 percent of the time for his portfolio just to break even after accounting for the costs of mistakes and the cost of buying and selling the securities. The funds sound like a simple answer to maximizing your returns, but market-timing decisions that are driven by greed or fear are frequently wrong.

General characteristics of well-managed asset allocation funds are high potential for capital growth, moderate current income and low to moderate stability of principal.

Growth and Income Funds

This is the largest family of funds in total consumer investment, and they are considered to be a conservative way to invest in the stock market and yet realize the market's overall gains. The name comes from the anticipated growth in the price of the stocks and the income from the stocks' dividends. Typically, growth and income funds invest in stocks of big, blue-chip, dividend-paying companies.

General characteristics are moderate potential capital growth, low to moderate current income and moderate stability of principal.

Index Stock Funds

Index mutual funds have no high-priced stock pickers, and in fact make no effort to pick winning stocks. Instead, they simply invest in all the stocks that make up the index in the same proportion that each stock makes up the overall index. The most popular stock index is the Standard & Poor's 500 stock index, which is dominated by large blue-chip companies. The index is made up of 88 groups of four major segments of the economy. It has 385 industrial stocks, 45 utility stocks, 55 financial stocks and 15 transportation stocks representing about 70 percent of the market value of all publicly traded stocks.

Standard & Poor's also has a 400 stock index composed of 400 midsize companies with capital of around $500 million. The other popular stock indexes are the Wilshire 5000 index, which includes the S&P 500 stocks plus 4,500 other stocks, and the Dow Jones Industrial 30 stock index.

The goal of index funds is to earn a rate of return that corresponds closely to the overall return on the stock market. Earning an average return is not all that shabby, especially when you consider that about 80 percent of all equity funds, after deducting sales charges and expenses, fail to equal the overall stock market average return.

General characteristics are moderate potential for capital growth, low current income and moderate stability of principal.

Growth Funds

These funds seek growth in the price of the stock rather than current income. They usually invest in well-established companies where the company and the industry are considered to have good long-term growth potential. They tend to avoid the less stable smaller companies that may provide substantial short-term gains at the risk of substantial declines later. While investors in these funds face greater short-term price volatility, those who can put their heads in the sand and wait out the long-term stock market cycles can reap better returns than they might with the average growth and income fund.

General characteristics are high to moderate potential for capital growth, low current income and low stability of principal.

Aggressive Growth Funds

This family of funds is for risk takers who seek maximum capital gains. Because the funds invest in stocks with high potential for rapid growth and capital appreciation, such as small emerging growth companies or undervalued blue-chip stocks, the returns can skyrocket on a rising stock market. On the other hand, they can experience wide swings in price and have a relatively low stability of principal. Aggressive growth funds can also boost returns—and risks—by borrowing, selling short, buying options and using other speculative strategies to leverage results. These funds can invest in any high-growth stock, or they may concentrate on one specific industry, in which case they are called *sector funds*.

General characteristics are very high potential for capital growth, low current income and low to very low stability of principal.

From 1972 to 1991, with dividends reinvested, conservative growth and income funds returned on average almost 11 percent each year. Moderate risk funds, such as growth funds, returned almost 13 percent, and aggressive growth funds about 14 percent. The S&P 500 returned about 12 percent over this period.

Other Popular Funds

Utility Funds

Many years ago, before the widespread use of mutual funds, utility stocks were referred to as "widow and orphan" stocks. The reason? Utilities, with a monopoly in their service area, continued to make money year in and year out. Over the past five years, they have returned about a 5 percent annual dividend yield and about 6 percent capital gains in the price of the stock. This makes utility stock funds a good "halfway house" for people who want to invest in the stock market but are reluctant to give up the safety of a savings account.

Now, another word from the real world. Conservative utility stocks, which are often suggested for income-seeking retirees, have soared 300 percent over the past ten years ending October 1, 1993, as compared to only 220 percent for the average stock mutual fund, according to Lipper Analytical Services. Over the past five years, they were up 105 percent versus 97 percent for the average fund.

Utility stocks may be considered a conservative investment, but they are also stocks with a major play on interest rates and inflation. When interest rates spike up, utility stocks can decline in value because they borrow huge amounts of money. But history tells us that the risk is low over any longer period of time.

Specialty Mutual Funds

The mutual fund industry offers funds for almost any investor. There are small company emerging growth funds that invest in stocks of young, growing companies; blue-chip funds that invest only in stocks of America's largest companies and international funds that invest in foreign stocks. This last group of funds offers a choice of where the investments are made, such as Latin America, Asia or Europe. Global funds invest around the world, including the United States. Sector funds invest primarily in one industry, such as gold mining, real estate, bio-tech, computer and high-tech companies.

How Much Will You Earn?

When you invest in a stock mutual fund, you don't know what you'll earn. Since no one knows what the future will bring, mutual fund advertising is based on past performance. The past performance, in turn, is illustrated as total returns. Here's what you commonly see in an advertisement: "Total returns for the period shown above are historical and include the reduction for sales charges, changes in share prices, reinvestment of dividends and capital gains. Past performance is no guarantee of future results. Share price and return will vary, and you may have a gain or loss when you sell your shares."

If you based your purchase on the past total returns of the fund, it's important to note that these returns may not occur in the future, and they are shown on the basis that you make no withdrawals from the fund. For example, when interest rates have fallen sharply, the total returns for bond funds can soar. If rates rise in the next year, the total returns can be sharply reduced or may even result in a negative total return. If the stock market soars one year and takes a dive the next, the total return will change accordingly.

Fund Ratings

Morningstar, the major mutual fund rating service, determines its ratings by comparing each fund's total return for three-year, five-year and ten-year periods with the average returns for its investment category. To measure risk, each fund's monthly performance is compared with that of risk-free three-month Treasury bills and then with the average for its investment category. Funds with a shorter track record than three years are not ranked. Each fund is awarded from one to five stars, with five stars the highest rating.

On average, about 35 percent of the funds receive three stars, the bottom 10 percent one star and the top 10 percent five stars. A five-star rating can mean that the fund had superior performance and was relatively low in risk compared to the other funds in its category. (Morningstar, 53 W. Jackson Blvd., Chicago, IL 60604, 800-876-5005.)

Fund ratings aren't perfect, and you should not buy a fund simply because it's rated four or five stars; however, the ratings do give you a guide as to where to start looking for a mutual fund. The funds know this as well. As with a new car that has just been named "Roadtrack Car of the Year," mutual funds also tout their star ratings. A recent ad pointed out that "the fund has earned the highest performance ratings of five stars from Morningstar since January 1992."

Beware of ads boasting that a fund is rated number one. The rankings might be from unrelated categories where the fund is competitive and leave out a lot of other funds with better performance records. Another ploy is to rank the fund with a few other funds of a certain size and select a short time period when the fund did well. According to a study of funds ranked by size, objective and time periods, 652 funds can be ranked number one at any given time.

Here are two ways a fund can make its long-term returns look better than they really are:

- Ten-year total returns. Every year begins a new ten-year period. For example, if the fund did poorly in 1983, a new ten-year period from 1984 to 1993 could substantially boost the ten-year total return.
- Selecting the best years. Many funds try to find the best performing years to highlight in their ads. The 1987 market crash is a good example. A fund's five-year performance no longer needs to include this downer year. A three-year period need no longer include the recession of 1990, in which funds dropped sharply in the second half of the year.

Before you take the "number one" rating at face value, check out the fine print in the ad to determine the number of funds in the group and the period on which the results are based.

Basic Rule #12:

Know what you'll pay in sales charges.

If you buy mutual fund shares from a broker or financial planner, you are likely to pay a sales fee. It's proper for them to charge a fee for their advice and help in finding the right fund that fits your need, but you should select a mutual fund with one eye on the costs. The problem today is that fund managers are becoming more imaginative in soaking the customer, making it harder for investors to know how much they will end up paying for the fund.

One area to check out is the fund's annual management fees, which come out of the hide of the investor. A good fund should have a management fee between 0.5 percent and 1 percent of the assets managed. Some funds have an annual management fee as low as 0.35 percent. The average stock fund has a management fee of about 1.5 percent. Some management fees, however, run as high as 2.5 percent or more. Here's how that can affect you. For example, suppose you invest $1,000, earning at least 5 percent a year, and you redeem the shares after three years. A good no-load fund, with a low management fee, might have a three-year expense projection of $17.60. Contrast that to a fund with an 8.5 percent sales commission with a high management fee and a three-year expense projection of $108.

You might think that a higher management fee means that the fund is better managed and will produce higher returns. These funds tout their high-priced stock pickers and their knowledge of the market, but they seldom offer returns that justify their hefty fees. According to Morningstar, from October 31, 1987, to October 31, 1992, a no-load stock fund with a 1.13 percent annual expense ratio had an annualized total return of 13.5 percent. A front-end load stock fund with a management fee of 1.3 percent had an annualized total return of 12.76 percent, and a back-end load fund, with a management fee of 2.16 percent had a total return of 12.2 percent.

Mutual Fund Fee Structures

As of last count, there are seven different ways mutual funds have found to reach into the fund buyer's pocket. These include an array of sales commissions, advertising fees and annual operating costs.

No-Load Funds

Called *true no-load funds,* these mutual funds are usually sold directly by the fund itself and have no sales charges when you buy or sell the investment. They have a low annual management fee of between 0.35 percent and 0.75 percent of the funds invested.

Low-Load Funds

These funds typically charge a front-end sales commission of up to 3 percent. Many of them were once no-load funds, so they are usually sold by mutual fund companies that also sell no-load funds. The funds may also have an exit fee, and they have an annual management fee of between 0.5 to 1 percent of the funds invested.

Load Funds

These funds carry a front-end sales commission of between 6.5 percent and 8 percent. Some funds also have an exit fee. These funds are usually sold by brokers, financial planners, banks and savings and loans. The average annual management fee is between 1.5 percent and 2 percent or more.

Back-End Load Funds

These funds tout the fact that you pay no up-front sales commission when you invest. They appear, and are often sold, as no-load funds, but before you smile all the way to the bank, consider this: The funds have a deferred sales load. No-load funds have historically been sold without a sales commission when you buy or sell, but if you sell a deferred-load fund within a specified number of years, typically six years, you pay a back-end sales charge on the entire amount you withdraw. The sales commission is downgraded each year you hold the fund. For example, if you cash out the investment after only one year, the sales charges might total 6 percent of the amount withdrawn. The sales commission typically declines by 1 percent each year you hold the investment and disappears altogether after six years.

Deferred-load funds are a way for brokers, financial planners and banks to earn a commission while selling so-called "no-load" funds. You may pay hefty sales charges if you withdraw your money in the earlier years because the fund needs to earn back the commissions it paid to the selling broker. These funds also may include trailer commissions. They are paid each year to the broker and trail the original sale. Many of these deferred-load funds also have astronomically high annual management expense fees. One fund had a whopping expense ratio of 2.3 percent per year. By comparison, Vanguard, which sells a comparable true no-load fund, has an expense ratio of only 0.35 percent.

12(b)1 Funds

Any fund, even funds without front-end sales commissions, can levy annual 12(b)1 fees. These funds ask shareholders to pay annual fees for the marketing and advertising expenses, known as *distribution fees*. The funds are known as "pay forever" funds because each year the fund charges marketing, advertising and other sales costs against the investor's fund balance. The funds typically have an exit fee for selling within the first year. Today, about 40 percent of equity funds carry 12(b)1 fees.

Pay-Later Funds

Many funds offer to temporarily absorb part or all of their annual management fees to increase returns to new buyers. This makes the fund more attractive, but the management fee can be reinstated at any time or after a short period as outlined in the offer. The funds figure that inertia will keep the new customers on the books after they once again slap on the management fees.

Pay-Now, Pay-Later Funds

Some funds charge not only a hefty up-front sales commission, but also sales charges every time you earn income that is credited to your account. Their shareholders face a no-win situation. If they withdraw the money to avoid the sales charges on reinvesting their dividends, they face hefty front-end sales commissions to reinvest with the same fund.

How obnoxious has the fee madness sweeping the industry become? Consider this: One brokerage firm's mutual fund has an annual management fee of 3.86 percent with a one-time sales commission as high as 6 percent!

You'll find commissions, annual management expenses and other fees in the fund's prospectus. It's a good idea to take a look before you jump in.

Industry Trends

Two major developments will change the way many people invest in mutual funds.

First, many previously true no-load funds are gradually becoming low-load funds. A low-load fund normally imposes a 3 percent front-end charge but has no sales charges when the funds are withdrawn. The fund managers say they need this extra income to offset the huge advertising, marketing and promotion costs to attract new investors.

Second, brokers and financial planners, who want to meet the competition from true no-load funds, will offer no-load funds with annual "trailer" commissions. For example, a broker who places $10,000 in a mutual fund with a 6 percent front-end load might receive a 4 percent first-year commission. That's $400 of income. On a no-load fund, the broker receives annual trailer commissions of 0.9 percent, or $90. However, unlike the front-end fund with a one-time commission, the trailer commissions continue for as long as the fund is held by the investor. Over ten years this can be a hefty return to the broker because the $10,000 original investment could increase to as much as $25,000, with the trailer commissions each year figured on the total amount of the assets under management.

Diversify To Reduce Risk

Market risk, interest rate risk and inflation risk are inherent in any investment, but mutual funds mitigate these risks through diversification. Even though a single mutual fund invests in many securities or stocks, I believe you should put your money into at least five different funds. If one of them underperforms the market, the others may score gains.

Like compounding, mutual funds are boring, but the bottom line is this: If you want to become wealthy, you need to invest a major portion of your assets in boring equity mutual funds and let time make you rich.

CHAPTER 4

Stick Your Head
in the Sand

*N*ow we come to another important lesson for building wealth. Wall Street is a giant casino, a game of chance, and anyone who claims to know how to predict the direction of the stock market or of an individual stock is simply blowing smoke in your ear. The truth is that no one knows when to buy or sell a stock, when to invest or stay on the sidelines. One of the oldest axioms on Wall Street is that "the market has a mind of its own."

Market Theories

Market-Timing Theory

The securities markets in the United States are open, free and competitive arenas in which large numbers of traders believe that a stock will rise or fall at the same time. The seller thinks it's time to take a profit, the buyer thinks hefty profits lie ahead. The idea, of course, is to determine who is right. In a perfectly efficient market, prices reflect what is known. In the actual stock market, prices often reflect the judgment of traders about current events and how these events, if they occur, will affect the market.

Random Walk Theory

One theory regarding the future of the stock market is that changes in stock prices will follow what is known on Wall Street as a "random walk." The random walk theory states that past prices are not a basis for forecasting future prices but, rather, that stock prices reflect reactions to information in a random fashion. Thus, future prices are no more predictable than a haphazard throw of the dice.

Technical Theory

The random walk theory is challenged by those who follow a technical analysis approach. Devotees of this method confidently predict the future of individual stocks and the stock market with charts of past stock prices. Known as technicians or chartists, they look at the advance-decline line, the cumulative total of advancing stocks minus declining stocks, the trading volume on the exchanges and when stocks hit new highs and lows. Working within the market itself, technicians try to predict the future from the past.

Fundamental Theory

On the other hand, those who follow fundamental analysis work outside the market. Called fundamentalists, they try to forecast stocks prices by analyzing the company's market share, balance sheet, products, management and the expected demand for the product or services. By using this method, fundamentalists believe they can tell when a stock or group of stocks is undervalued or overvalued at the current market price.

Based on these theories regarding the price movements of stocks, there is a never-ending supply of books and kits on how to make money in stocks. They purport to give you the inside story on the techniques used by professional traders. The authors say they know how to identify the numbers in a company balance sheet that every investor should be concerned about, how to read economic indicators that flash warning signals of market changes and how action in major stock groups foretells market turning points.

Market timers and stock pickers try to beat the average stock market returns. It may seem reasonable to believe that investors, using the latest market forecasting methods, or looking at the stars or moon, as we'll see later, should be able to achieve a better-than-average return. But from my years of experience I have concluded that both chartists and fundamentalists are clouding the real issue: The stock market has a mind of its own.

Basic Rule #13:

Stay in the market at all times.

The truth is, trying to outguess the direction of the stock market—picking stocks, buying and selling, timing—gets no better results on average than having an orangutan throw darts at newspaper stock tables stuck on the wall. Market timing is an illusion. No one can know when stock prices will rise or fall. No one, not brokers, financial planners, mutual fund managers, newsletter writers or I, can consistently buy low and sell high. Although market timers may reduce short-term risks by exiting the market when it declines, they lose hefty returns because they aren't fully invested when the market rallies.

"Experts'" Scorecard

Investment Newsletters

Mark Hulbert, who writes the *Hulbert Financial Digest*, a newsletter that tracks the results from hundreds of investment newsletters, says, "The primary virtue of market-timing newsletters isn't beating the market. In fact, their virtue lies in their ability to reduce risk by more than return, which is forfeited in the process. This is not a realistic goal, however, because market timers also are trying to reduce risk." One way to reduce risk is to invest only half in stocks and hold the balance in cash, but Hulbert cautions that with this strategy your rate of return would also be about half as much as the market's.

Hulbert says that although market timers do reduce some risk, over the past 16 years, to August 1993, only 16.7 percent of timers actually beat a buy-and-hold strategy, and, over the past 5 years, only 10.9 percent. (*Hulbert Financial Digest*, 316 Commerce St., Alexandria, VA 22314, 703-683-5905.)

James Schmidt, editor of *The Timer Digest*, a newsletter that tracks the performance of market-timing newsletters, bases the performance of the letters on the S&P 500 stock index, which is set at 100.00 at the start of the period. The S&P 500 is a broad-based measurement of the changes in stock market prices based on the average performance of 500 widely held common stocks. For the period August 1992 to August 1993, during which the S&P 500 climbed to 109.06, only five of the letters managed to beat it, with the top performer at 112.84. From October 1992 to October 1993, only four newsletters, with an average index of 112.50, beat the S&P 500 value of 110.81. (*The Timer Digest*, Box 1688, Greenwich, CT 06836, 203-629-3503.)

The so-called "market experts" who write the investment newsletters try every imaginable device to become *The Timer Digest*'s number one long-term timer of the year. In 1992, this distinction went to Arch Crawford, who writes *Crawford Perspectives*.

His secret of knowing when to buy and sell stocks? He times the market with astrology. He picks buy-and-sell opportunities by using a combination of planetary cycles with the moon and stars. In a recent issue, Crawford tells his readers, "We forecast an extreme solar event, and skies will light up with massive harmonic planetary aspects. The very next day, a new moon at perigee (closest passage to the Earth) creates the exact worst combination. Watch for abnormalities in weather, earthquakes and financial markets." Crawford warns that the position of Mars can also portend tight money and a currency crisis. (*Crawford Perspectives*, 1456 Second Ave., Suite 145, New York, NY 10021, 212-535-6202.)

With investors lacking any other successful method of picking stocks, the age of financial astrology is on the upswing. There is even an astrologer's mutual fund for those who believe sunspots translate into selloffs.

Many newsletter writers and brokers love to tout the hottest stocks in the market, telling tales of huge profits that await the savvy investor. However, a study by the Babson Group of mutual funds found that the hottest stock on the market in each of the past 11 years, stocks that many investors fell all over themselves to buy, have performed miserably. More than half of them actually declined in price while the S&P 500 stock index doubled.

The fall of these so-called "hot" stocks was no accident. The companies were often at the cutting edge of a new technology or a new type of business when their stocks skyrocketed. In every instance, the promise of rapid growth brought many competitors into these companies' markets, soon diminishing their seemingly brilliant prospects. When you invest in these high-flyer stocks, remember that most of the wonderful things that such exciting companies could achieve in the future have already been reflected in the price of their stock. Once a stock is recognized as a wave of the future, there's a good chance it could drown you.

Despite their sorry track record of predicting the next hot stock and when to buy and sell, the investment newsletter writers never quit. And why should they? At an average cost of some $250 a year, they continue to make money telling eager investors how and when to buy and sell on Wall Street. Are high-priced investment newsletters worthwhile? Mark Hulbert, writing in *Forbes* (June 7, 1993), says that, based on his study, "There is absolutely no correlation between higher price and better performance. If anything, it is just the reverse. Over the past five years, the 20 percent of letters with the lowest subscription fees had the best average performance. These inexpensive newsletters produced a compound annual return of 15.2 percent. In contrast, those letters in the costliest price range returned 10.5 percent." During this same period, the overall stock market had an annual return of 15.4 percent.

One monthly newsletter, which between issues provided a telephone hot line with daily updates, at an annual cost of $995, was no bargain. If you had followed its advice over the years, you would have failed to earn even the Treasury bill rate. Another investment letter with a subscription cost of $650 a year actually lost 77 percent over the past five years on its portfolio of futures recommendations.

A disturbing trend has developed among some investment newsletters. In an attempt to lower costs, many have turned into little more than hidden advertising messages for financial firms. One major letter says, "Enclosures are paid advertisements. The newsletter is not endorsing any specific company or product. This revenue defrays the cost of producing this newsletter and mailing to you." Another notes that, "As you are aware, inserts carried in this newsletter are paid for by fee and commission. This helps to keep our subscription rates down while enabling us to maintain the quality of services to our subscribers." When you are paying big bucks for help on where to invest, I don't believe you should have to wade through paid commercials to learn what the writer has to say, and then wonder how objective he or she is.

Pension Fund Managers

If newsletters for the average investor can't outguess the market, what about pension fund managers working with billions of dollars? In its October 25, 1993, issue entitled "Money Business," *Forbes* found that American business spends $9 billion a year on money managers for their employee pension plans—and most of the spending is futile. One 1992 study from the Brookings Institution shows that the average professional investment manager lagged behind the S&P 500 stock index by 2.6 percent per year over seven years. A good part of this lag, *Forbes* says, can be traced not to stupidity or incompetence, but to the simple fact that trading stocks and supervising money managers costs money. The question *Forbes* asks is, "Why shouldn't the average American company just fire its squadrons of money managers and put its pension money into an index fund with low turnover and minimal fees?" As one expert put it: "It's like monkeys trading bananas in trees. The money managers end up with a lot of bananas."

Stockbrokers

Can you trust your broker to tell you when and what to buy? Like everyone else in the business of predicting stock prices, brokers are right about as often as the roll of the dice. This recommendation of one stock picker who uses the fundamental analysis approach appeared in a broker's report:

> We believe that the recent weakness in the price of most stocks presents a buying opportunity rather than an excuse to raise cash. In our opinion, the underlying fundamentals have not changed sufficiently to warrant a more cautious attitude toward equities. With the price of most stocks down to varying degrees, it is timely to seek out those with relatively solid fundamentals that have been caught in the market's downdraft, along with issues with relatively less attractive prospects.

If the brokerage firm has a "buy" on a stock, what you may not know is that a buy signal is usually a recommendation to hold. If the brokerage firm downgrades the stock to a "hold," that's a subtle way of saying sell. And Wall Street's version of a sell signal often can be translated into the fact that you should have been out of the stock a week ago.

A growing number of studies tell the same story. In one demonstration on ABC's "20/20," the host actually threw darts at the stock tables on the wall during the program and beat the expert's predictions. The *Wall Street Journal* runs a contest that pits professional stock pickers against dart throwers in which the dart throwers have won about half the time.

The lesson in this is that making money in the stock market is easy. It's boring, but it's easy. You just have to invest in good-performing equity mutual funds and then, like an ostrich, stick your head in the sand and ignore the stock market. The bad news and flameouts on Wall Street can't hurt you. What can hurt you is your panic in trying to do something about financial bad news. If you learn to stay in the stock market at all times, through market crashes and record Dows, what you paid for this book will be returned to you many times over.

Here's a classic example. In the summer of 1929 a young man, at his father's suggestion, put the $400 he had earned on odd jobs into a mutual fund. Almost before the ink was dry on his investment receipt, the biggest stock market crash in history shattered Wall Street. By 1933, the value of his investment had fallen to just $85. With this kind of loss, he decided to stay in the market, but he never put any more money in what appeared to him a losing proposition. Today, his original $400 investment is worth more than $40,000.

Secret of Success: Stand Pat

The secret of this individual's success was that he stayed in the stock market at all times. No one knows in advance when to be in or out of the market, but the rewards for the courageous who stay in can be breathtaking. More than 95 percent of the gain in the stock market in an average year can occur in just a few trading days. Here's how your annual return can be affected if you're not invested at all times:

The Bull Market from 1982 to 1987

Time in the Stock Market	Average Annual Total Return with Dividends Reinvested
Invested for all 1,276 trading days	26.3%
Out of the market the best 20 days	13.1%
Out of the market the best 40 days	4.3%

Note that if you were out of the market for only the best 40 trading days during this five-year period, your average annual return fizzled to just 4.3 percent, nearly the same as a money market return.

I've talked on the air with Bill Berger, president of the Berger Funds of Denver, Colorado, about his long career in building shareholders' wealth. Bill knows the value of staying in the market at all times. He says, "You can liken the situation to a man walking his dog. He's going from point A to point B by following a path of growing earnings. His dog, much like the stock market, is running off in different directions, chasing a rabbit, barking at a squirrel. The man is too wise to wear himself out following the dog; he knows the dog, and the stock market, will be with him at point B when he gets there."

Basic Rule #14:

The average stock mutual fund can't beat the overall stock market.

Everyone would like a peek at tomorrow's financial pages. The next best thing, you might guess, is to invest in a stock mutual fund with an array of high-priced stock pickers who often pop up on television telling you what to buy and sell. You've heard them explain where the market is headed. It might sound like this: "We think the improvement in the market is sustainable at this time. The rebound probably reflects a fundamental improvement in the financial services, so we'd be buyers in these industries and sell any holdings we had in auto stocks."

Do they really know what stocks to buy or where the market is headed? Chances are they don't. The expert stock pickers of the average equity mutual fund can beat the overall stock market averages only about 10 to 15 percent of the time. Lipper Analytical Services studied how the performance of the average stock mutual fund compared to the S&P 500 stock index to October 1, 1992. Here's a summary of the findings:

Holding Period	*Total Return*	
	Average Stock Fund	*S&P 500 Index*
1 year	8.24%	11.04%
5 years	45.18%	53.89%
10 years	292.64%	403.29%

Of course, this comparison is for the "average" fund. Better-performing mutual funds do beat the market averages by a significant amount, sometimes as much as double the average total returns. The trick is to pick the better-performing funds rather than trying to outguess the market or an individual stock.

The good news for those who stay in the market at all times is that the Dow Jones Industrial Average has continued to rise over the years. Sometimes we forget just how fast the Dow (and the stock market) has been soaring. At the start of 1982, the Dow was about 800. By 1987, just before the market crash, it was about 2600. In the worst market selloff since the Great Depression, when the Dow tumbled more than 500 points, it recovered its previous level by the middle of 1989 and, by the end of 1992, it stood at 3200. A year later the Dow was over 3700. That's a gain of 2,900 points from 1982 to 1993! If the Dow can gain about 8 percent a year, less than its previous yearly gains over the past decade, it will be at 6000 by the year 2000—six years from now.

What risk do you run by staying in the market at all times? If you stay in the stock market or in a stock mutual fund for only one year, you can run a significant risk. The performance of common stocks between 1926 and 1992 has varied from a best annual return of 54 percent to a worst loss of 43 percent. However, through periods of high inflation, market crashes and wars, one important point is clear: The longer you hold stocks, the less chance you run of losing money. Over a ten-year period, for example, the risk of owning stocks has been almost zero.

Two of the oldest mutual funds in America have never had a loss in any ten-year period. To put it another way, no shareholders in these funds who left their investments alone for ten years have ever lost money. The two funds are the State Street Investment Trust, started in 1924, and the Pioneer Fund, started in 1928.

These funds bore the full brunt of the 1929 stock market crash and the subsequent Great Depression, and they went through the prolonged bear market of the mid-1970s, when stocks as a whole lost 40 percent in two years. The worst ten years for both funds was 1928 to 1937, during which time they had about a 23 percent total return. Throughout the postwar years, investors who put their heads in the sand and invested for ten years generally more than tripled their money. The average ten-year return since 1924 has been 10.9 percent: $1,000 invested then would be worth $4 million now.

On a more recent note, take the averages of the Dow Jones Industrials for the past ten years, from 1984 to 1993. During this period, the Dow reflected the stock market: It went up and down. To earn the best return over this period, it was important not only to stay in the market at all times, but to continue to invest regularly.

In 1984, the Dow was down 3.7 percent. The next year, however, it was up a hefty 27.7 percent, up again by 22.6 percent in 1986, and up only 2.3 percent in 1987. In 1988, the gain was 11.9 percent; in 1989, a whopping 27 percent. The Dow was down by 4.3 percent in 1990, but it made up for lost ground in 1991 with a gain of 20.3 percent. In 1992, the Dow was up only 4.2 percent and in 1993, it was up 13.7 percent. The overall average annual gain during this ten-year period in the Dow was 12.17 percent.

Not all years were winners; losses did occur in 1984 and 1990, while in four years the Dow gained 20 percent or more. If the past is any indicator, to match the stock market returns in the future, you don't need good-luck charms and the assurance of a fortune teller, you just need common sense to stay invested at all times and the guts to avoid the temptation of the latest "hot" investment tip.

On the other hand, avoiding an investment in the stock market because of the chance of a loss is a little like avoiding a train ride because of a possible wreck. Life is full of uncertainties, but investing long term in the stock market is not one of them. You will make money investing in stocks if you give the market enough time to do the job.

CHAPTER 5

Building a Nest Egg

*I*f you equate finding a mutual fund with a visit to a dentist for a root canal, you're not alone. Before financial deregulation, an insured certificate of deposit was a fixed savings account, and a Treasury bill was a Treasury bill. At least you knew what you were buying. Not any more. Today, with the floodgates open and the computers whirling out new investment products each day, it's not what's best for the investor, but what will sell that has become important. As a result, the number of specialty mutual funds is exploding.

Mutual Fund Mania

One of the latest specialty mutual funds advances the economic and social status of women. It invests in companies that have a high percentage of female executives and directors, offer family-oriented benefits such as child care and contribute to organizations that promote women's independence. Another new one is the China

World Fund, which invests in fledgling companies in that country that are expected to grow faster than those in the United States. The problem with all these new headline-grabbing funds is that you may not know what you've invested in until you take a loss. I believe that most investors need to develop an investment portfolio that is built on well-established, proven stock equity mutual funds invested in American companies.

The first step in building your long-term nest egg is to learn that brokers, investment advisers and banks have a product to sell. Think of a brokerage house as a supermarket of money with a back room filled with unsold products. You may not find red-tag sales on the mutual funds and bonds, but just as in the supermarket, the brokers and financial planners have to move out the products if the salespeople are to eat. With today's competition, not every broker or financial adviser will find a full meal because new players have invaded their turf.

In recent years, consumers have been pulling their savings out of low-yielding bank accounts at record rates and investing in mutual funds without ever leaving the bank. Banks and savings and loans are pursuing every imaginable ploy in their intensive marketing battle to sell their customers mutual funds. A major bank is even offering mutual funds through its automatic teller machines. Other banks, which boast that Wall Street has come to their local branches, have attractive "investment centers" in the lobby, a short walk from the tellers' windows. Unfortunately, many bank customers making this walk believe that anything sold in a bank is insured and as riskless as a savings account. A recent Securities and Exchange Commission (SEC) survey of 1,000 investors who bought mutual funds at a bank rather than from a broker or financial planner found that 20 percent of them thought mutual funds sold through banks were federally insured, and 10 percent didn't know. Forty-one percent thought mutual funds sold by the bank were backed by the bank's assets, and 19 percent didn't know. Mutual funds sold by banks carry the same risks as those sold by brokers and financial planners.

According to the banking industry, about 3,500 banks—about one-third of all banks—sell mutual funds. They currently offer about 1,200 funds, up from only 210 funds five years ago. What you may not know is that, in an effort to hang onto the depositor's money, about a third of all new mutual fund sales in 1993 were made by banks and savings and loans. The American Bankers Association predicts that within a few years banks will sell half of all mutual funds.

While many banks sell so-called "branded" funds, such as Kemper and Putnam, several larger banks have also developed their own families of mutual funds. In 1993, there were 110 bank-sponsored mutual funds. New York's Citibank, for example, offers customers some 600 mutual funds besides its own family of funds. Bank of America's Pacific Horizon funds and Chase Manhattan Bank's Vista funds have performed very well, and some of their funds rank at or near the top in recent mutual fund performance. Not all bank mutual funds do as well. Banks tend to be more conservative in managing their funds because most of their customers are averse to risk and want funds that provide low price volatility and stable growth.

In a further effort to grab mutual fund sales, The Mellon Bank will acquire Dreyfus, the country's sixth-largest mutual fund company. This requires some fancy legal footwork to sidestep the depression-era Glass-Steagall Act, which prohibits banks from sponsoring a mutual fund, but loopholes in the act make it easy for banks to enter the mutual fund business. Banks will continue to move away from the traditional banking business of taking deposits and making loans. For example, Mellon expects with the acquisition of Dreyfus to receive 60 percent of its revenue from fees rather than from interest payments on loans.

New Marketing Strategies

Brokers and financial planners face yet another competitor: the big mutual funds. The mutual fund industry is about to get a new game plan in which the investor can buy a fund simply by responding to an advertisement in a magazine or newspaper and mailing in a coupon with a check. This bypasses the broker and financial planner by allowing the investor to deal directly with the funds.

The SEC, the government agency that regulates the securities business, refers to this as "off-the-page" marketing, or investing in a fund directly from ads that include a summary prospectus. It used to be that you invested in a mutual fund only after you received a full prospectus outlining the fund's operations, commissions and objectives. Reading a prospectus is a good idea, but almost no one does it. A Wall Street trader told me years ago that, "It's no wonder people don't read the prospectuses. They're written like a used-car warranty in Greek."

With off-the-page marketing the mutual fund companies will fill their ads with attractive numbers. Some will tilt the ads in their favor, while others are sure to resort to deceptive advertising. The sales hype is there to put a happy face on the products the funds want to sell, but savvy investors understand that they are not being told the whole story.

Here are the questions to ask before you invest through summary prospectus advertising:

- Is the fund a no-load, low-load, regular-load or back-end load, and does it charge 12b-1 fees? Does the fund charge a sales commission when you reinvest the dividends?
- What are the fund's annual management fees, 12b-1 fees and other charges? The advertisement should indicate the expenses a typical investor would pay on a $1,000 investment for one, three, five and ten years.
- What are the fund's possible risks and goals?
- What kinds of securities does the fund invest in, and what amount does it already have in each category? If the fund calls itself a government securities fund, for example, what percentage of its assets are actually invested in government bonds?
- What is the minimum investment and minimum additional investment, and what are the restrictions and costs, if any, for redeeming shares?

To be a successful investor you need to understand what is really important in these newspaper and magazine ads and what is just window dressing. In 1993, when insured CDs were yielding less than 3 percent, a huge mutual fund ran a full-page advertisement on its growth and income fund. The big headlines proclaimed an "average total annual return of 26.88 percent from 12-31-91 to 6-30-93, and one year, 18.58 percent." These are hefty returns indeed, but the ad didn't tell the prospective investor that the returns for 1993 were a great deal less than in the previous years, and the year-to-date figures were even lower.

Basic Rules for Investing

As you build your nest egg, remember these important points *before* you plunk down your money:

1. When interest rates are expected to rise, don't go long term. Keep the maturities within one year for CDs and about five to seven years for bonds. You may not earn top interest rates, but you won't get killed with hefty price declines later on when bond yields do rise.
2. Ask about the possible changes in the market value of your fixed-income investment. All the soothing talk about guarantees and safety won't ease your aggravation when you discover that the current value of your investment, should you sell, is now far less than it was when you bought it.
3. Find out how soon you can get your money back and at what cost. Your life can change, emergencies can pop up, and you don't want to find that you're handcuffed with hefty redemption costs when you need the money.

   A good example of this possibility is investing in a tax-deferred annuity. Your financial advisers may tell you that it's a good deal—that you can avoid sales commissions when you invest and delay taxes until retirement. That may be true, but look at what it can cost you if you need the money in a year. First, if you're under the age of 59 1/2, you'll pay a 10 percent tax penalty on all the money you withdraw. Then, since you did not pay a sales commission when you bought the annuity, you could face a back-end load of as much as 8 percent. That's a whopping 18 percent off the top in one year just to get your original investment back.

4. Don't invest short term for long-term goals. If you are saving for the expenses of a college education, you probably already know that the college costs are rising at more than twice the inflation rate. If your child has five years to go before attending college, plan on spending at least $15,000 a year; if ten years, at least $20,000. How in the world can you save for this future expense with a savings account earning 4 percent a year? By the time you pay income taxes on what you earned, you're adding to your college fund at less than half the rise in tuition alone. To see how fast you are saving money for college expenses, use the banker's *rule of 72*. Take the number 72 and divide it by the rate of return you're getting on a savings account. That will tell you how long it will take to double your money. If the rate is 4 percent, the grim answer is 18 years—long after your child may have graduated from college. If you can earn 6 percent on a fixed-income investment, it will still take you 12 years to double your money. If you invest in a stock mutual fund with annual returns of about 15 percent, your money will double in only about five years.

   Let's be honest. You simply can't send your kids to college with a safe, guaranteed, low-yielding savings account.

5. Don't invest in anything you don't understand. Ask for the material you need and study it carefully. Ask as many questions as you like; after all, it's your money. Put your investment objectives in writing, and go over them with your broker or financial planner. That way you can learn whether or not your adviser understands what kind of investments you want. In too many cases, the broker is a salesperson who is on the phone all day talking to clients and prospects, reading about the latest offering from the firm and placing orders.

6. Cut your losses. If you buy stocks from a broker or financial planner, follow the old Wall Street saying: Let your profits run and cut your losses. Many brokers cut the profits to sell the customer another stock and let the losses run. Some investors can't admit that they made an error in buying a stock in the first place. They become emotionally involved

with an investment and hold on in the hope that they'll break even. A better plan is to set a target price at which you would sell the stock. If the stock price goes up, you can adjust your target price upward. If the price goes down, quickly sell the stock. It's easy to know when to sell. Ask yourself: Would I buy the stock again today? If the answer is no, consider selling it.

If you invest in common stocks that are traded on an exchange, be sure you understand a *stop order to sell*. To a securities broker, a stop order to sell is an order to sell a stock at a specified price or better (called the stop-limit price) but only after the stop price has been reached or passed. For example, say you buy 100 shares of XYZ Corporation at $40 a share. Instead of watching the price of XYZ stock on a daily basis, or to protect yourself from a stock market crash, you can place a stop order to sell at $36 a share. If the price of XYZ takes a nosedive, your stop order will be triggered as close to $36 a share as possible, and the broker will sell the stock.

The risk in stop orders is that they can be triggered by a temporary market movement. After you've sold the XYZ stock at $36, you might find that the market recovers and the price of the stock soars to $41. But if you don't watch the stock market on a daily basis and tend to become paralyzed during a major market selloff, stop orders can prevent having to sell the XYZ stock at $25 a share a month later.

Basic Rule #15:

Build a model investment portfolio.

Part of your overall financial plan will be to design a portfolio that fits your lifestyle, your needs and your tolerance for risk. Therefore, your portfolio should change as you advance toward retirement. Here are the basic steps you need to take:

Step 1: Decide How You're Going To Divide Your Investments

You should divide your investments between short-term, income-oriented plans and long-term equity investments. Short-term investing can be used for current income, emergency money and short-term savings objectives such as a new car, a down payment on a home or a vacation. Long-term investing should be for retirement and college.

Consider your time horizon. Separate each segment of your overall investment plan. Are you saving for retirement? For the costs of a college education? For the down payment on a home? Generally, the longer the time frame, the more aggressive you can be. For example, if you're saving for a down payment on a home in one or two years, you'll want to invest conservatively in fixed-income savings plans or bonds. You want the money safe and available when you need to write the check. For your retirement in 15 or 20 years, you can sock away the money in stock funds where you can afford to be more venturesome and take higher risks for greater long-term returns.

Step 2: Decide How You're Going To Diversify Your Investments

The allocation of your assets is one of the most important steps you can take to boost your retirement income. How you make this allocation between savings accounts, bonds and stocks will depend on your age, your risk tolerance and your willingness to move your assets among these investments.

The key to building a portfolio is to determine the amount of risk you can take and still feel comfortable. As a general rule, the greater the risk, the greater the potential returns. There are four basic groups of investments:

- Aggressive growth. This high-risk group includes aggressive growth stocks or mutual funds, small-cap stocks or stock funds, high-yield "junk bonds," commodities and options.

- Growth. This more conservative group includes balanced funds and growth and income funds that invest in blue-chip companies, preferred stocks, utility stocks and stock funds.
- Stability of principal with income. This conservative group includes municipal bonds and bond funds, fixed-income bond funds, high-quality major corporate bonds or bond funds, zero coupon bonds and U.S. Treasury securities.
- Safety of principal. This group includes the safest investments you can make, such as FDIC-insured certificates of deposit, money market funds and short-term Treasury bills and notes.

One of the biggest mistakes investors make in their personal long-term financial planning is to put all or most of their money to work in the last group, seeking safety of principal. Unless you are retired and need the interest income for living expenses or are saving for a short-term goal, keep your super-safe investments to a minimum. The difference between 4 or 5 percent at the bank or in Treasury securities and 12 to 15 percent in stocks can mean the difference, over time, between a comfortable retirement or just getting by.

Most people make this same mistake when they allocate their investments in retirement plans. It makes no sense to have a fixed savings account in your company's 401(k) plan or your individual retirement account when you won't need the money until many years later.

Basic Rule #16:

Invest 100 minus your age in the stock market.

In building your portfolio, consider this rule for investing in equities. If you are 60, you should have at least 40 percent in stock funds or other equity investments. If you're 30, you should have at least 70 percent in stocks. This rule applies to both your retirement plan and your personal investing.

"Wait a minute," you say. "The stock market is risky." That's true. Equity mutual funds offer no guarantees. Their value can fluctuate up and down, and, in any one year, it's possible that you can lose money, but after stocks decline in any one year, they always go on to new highs. You should, therefore, invest in stock mutual funds for at least five years. Based on history, the chance of losing money during this period is almost zero.

Step 3: Decide How You're Going To Diversify in Each Category

As you diversify your assets, consider the total return for different asset allocations. According to Dimensional Fund Advisors, Inc., of Santa Monica, CA, the historical 20-year (1974 to 1993) annualized total returns for one-month Treasury bills was 7.49 percent; 20-year long bonds, 10.17 percent; S&P 500 large company stocks, 12.76 percent; and small company stocks, 17.70 percent.

Mutual funds are a great way to diversify your investments. They allow you to build a portfolio by selecting a wide range of different stock, bond and fixed-income funds. Therefore, don't invest in only one mutual fund, even though it may be one of the best on Wall Street. You need to spread your risk as you build your portfolio. This step may be unavoidable for new investors with fund minimums of $500 to $1,000, but as your nest egg grows, you should diversify into four or five funds.

Step 4: Build Your Own Portfolio

In asset allocation, there are three basic model portfolios: aggressive, moderate and conservative. For the most part, the portfolio you select will be a factor of your age. Of course, each individual's needs are different, so there are no fixed portfolios. You need to design one that fits your own situation.

Getting Started: Ages 20 to 30

This is a period for aggressive growth with a long time horizon to retirement. It may be the most difficult time to save and invest when you are just starting to acquire a home, car and other personal property. However, it's also the most critical time to start your investment program because a dollar invested today can bring the same rewards at retirement as $15 invested in mid-life.

For individual investing, you probably should be at least 75 to 80 percent in equities. For example, you might put 40 percent in growth stock funds, 20 percent in small-cap stock funds and 20 percent in international stock funds. The remaining 20 percent can be invested in fixed savings and bond funds.

For retirement investing in IRAs or 401(k) plans, at least 90 percent in equity stock funds, the remaining 10 percent in bond funds.

The object of this portfolio is maximum growth of principal, little if any cash income and capital preservation subordinate to growth over the longer term.

Family Years: Ages 30 to 50

At this stage in your life, you may have a growing family and still have 20 or more years to save for retirement. It's a time to scale back your risk level a bit while still seeking overall growth of your principal.

For individual investing, you'll want to put at least 50 to 60 percent in equities, diversifying with perhaps 40 percent in stock funds, 10 percent in small-cap funds and 10 percent in international funds. The remaining 40 percent could be invested in fixed-income investments, such as 25 percent in shorter-term bond funds, 10 percent in longer-term corporate bond funds and 5 percent in international bond funds.

For retirement investing in IRAs, 401(k) plans, at least 75 percent in equity stock funds and the balance in fixed-income bonds and other special opportunities with a five- or ten-year growth projection.

The object of this portfolio is primarily growth of principal with capital preservation, yet it should allow for the cash needs of a growing family.

Maximum Savings: Ages 50 to 65

This period of your life will probably be your peak earning years. Your children may be grown and out of the house, and you can concentrate on the last leg of building your retirement security.

For individual investing, remembering the 100 minus your age rule, you should be at least 40 percent in equities, 30 percent in stock mutual funds and 10 percent in small-cap and international stocks. For fixed savings, a good mix would be 30 percent in income bond funds, 20 percent in Treasury securities and 10 percent in international bond funds.

For retirement investing in IRAs and 401(k) plans, continue to keep at least 60 percent of your assets in stock funds, with the balance in fixed savings accounts and longer-term corporate bond funds.

The objective of this portfolio is to continue to build your assets toward retirement with some degree of safety and to allow for unexpected cash needs prior to retirement.

Ready to Retire: Ages 65 plus

During this stage of your life, the monthly income you seek and the overall value of your portfolio will determine how you split your investments between fixed-income bonds and equity stock mutual funds. Most investors at this age typically have the greater part of their assets in safer fixed-income bonds, but again, even if you are in retirement and you don't plan to use some of the money for four or five years, you need the inflation protection of stocks to maintain the spending power of your assets.

For individual investing, you should have about 60 percent in bonds or fixed-income funds, depending on your current cash needs, 30 percent in stock funds and 10 percent in international stock funds or special opportunities.

For retirement investing in IRAs and 401(k) plans, a good division would be 40 percent in equity stock funds and 60 percent in bond funds and savings accounts. The objective of this portfolio is maximum capital preservation with some growth of principal to overcome the effects of inflation and to provide the cash needs in retirement.

Dollar Cost Averaging

After you've determined your portfolio makeup and allocated your investments between stocks, bonds and fixed savings, you must try to continue adding to your equity investments. Don't waste time trying to find the perfect moment to jump into the stock market; dollar cost averaging is as close as you can come to infallible investing.

Over the long term, it slants the odds in your favor when you invest a fixed amount each month. Most financial books don't even talk about dollar cost averaging, and most people have never heard of it. The idea behind dollar cost averaging is that you are not only forced to invest regularly, to pay yourself first, but, since you buy fund shares at different prices over time, you tend to average out the cost.

Let's suppose that you can invest $100 a month in the ABC Fund. In the first month, if ABC's shares are selling at $10, you'd buy 10 shares. If the price falls to $5 a share in the next month, you'd buy 20 shares. The following month, ABC Fund's share price might climb back to $7.50, and you'd buy 13.3 shares. Then, in the fourth month, ABC shares might soar to $12.50 a share, and you'd buy 8 shares.

In the four-month period, you invested a total of $400. You purchased 51.3 shares at an average share price of about $7.80. Therefore, the total cost of your investment is $400. This example of dollar cost averaging will give you a general idea of how it works, even though the average mutual fund share price may change very little from month to month. The advantage of dollar cost averaging is that not only do you continue to invest each month to build up your nest egg, but the average cost per share can be lower than the average price per share. A friend of mine said he likes dollar cost averaging because when share prices are low, he can buy more shares, and when they are expensive, he buys fewer shares.

Dividend Reinvestment

When you invest in mutual funds, make sure you ask the fund management to reinvest your dividends by purchasing additional shares. This is another form of dollar cost averaging. What's more, you should be able to avoid sales commissions because the income is already inside the fund. The long-term effect of reinvesting dividends is that you take full advantage of the awesome power of compounding to boost your total assets when you want to spend the money in retirement.

Here's an example of how reinvesting dividends each year can boost your retirement nest egg: Assume you make a one-time investment of $10,000 in a stock mutual fund that earns 15 percent each year. (The 1983–1992 ten-year average annual return of the S&P 500 stock index was 16.8 percent.) Also assume the dividend rate each year is 3 percent.

Years Invested	Withdrawing Dividends	Reinvesting Dividends
5 years	$17,623	$ 20,114
10 years	31,058	40,456
15 years	54,736	81,371
20 years	96,463	163,665

Reinvesting dividends can create wealth on a scale that defies imagination. After 5 years, you've doubled your original investment, after 10 years you've doubled it again, after 15 years you've doubled it again, and after 20 years your $10,000 investment can provide over $160,000 in retirement spending.

Sit on Your Hands after You Invest

After you've built your model portfolio with a few good stock funds and kept some of the money in government or blue-chip bond funds and fixed savings, then it's important to sit on your hands and hope that history will repeat itself with a continuing upward movement of the stock market. Will it? I think it will. It has done so for the past 60 years. History has shown that time is your greatest ally. Whatever your age, if you start now to build a portfolio, I guarantee you'll have a better retirement income, and be much less likely to run out of money before you run out of breath.

CHAPTER 6

The Cost of Credit Cards

Do you know what the number one sport in America is today? According to most experts who follow consumer trends, it's not baseball. It's shopping. Americans have become impulse shoppers, filling their closets and garages with little-used items while they max out on their credit cards. Credit counselors now say that for many people, credit card debt no longer means a $2,000 balance on one card. Rather, they often see debts of $40,000 or more on up to 20 different credit cards.

There are now more than a billion credit cards in circulation nationwide—almost four cards for every American citizen—and credit card debt during the plastic prosperity of the 1980s soared to almost $270 billion, triple that of a decade earlier. Today, card-holders pay an average of $440 in interest a year, or a total of $33 billion. To reap a hefty profit on this spending spree, the card issuers have kept the average credit card interest rate at over 16 percent.

Next time you set off for the shopping mall, be sure to remember this basic rule of good financial planning:

Basic Rule #17:

Avoid credit card debt.

Chargeaholics believe in living today and paying back tomorrow. The problem with this system is that when you borrow on your credit card, you are effectively borrowing against your future income. Just like the U.S. government, the more you borrow today, the more of your future income must be used to pay interest on your debt. I know, it's incredibly easy to use plastic instead of cash. People do it every day. But buying more than you can afford to pay off at the end of the month can preclude your saving any of your income first, and it takes a huge chunk out of your future wealth. One way to control spending is to cancel your credit cards and return to the days when people used cash and checks. Later in this chapter I'll offer some less painful strategies.

Types of Credit Cards

Credit cards come in two basic types. One is the travel and entertainment card, such as American Express and Shell Oil. These cards expect you to pay the balance in full each month. The other is the revolving credit card that allows you to "revolve" a portion of the balance by paying a minimum monthly amount, which includes finance charges.

Millions of Americans now find credit card solicitations cramming their mailboxes as new players try to steal customers from other credit card issuers. The offers come with "teaser" interest rates—lower initial rates for a set period—higher credit lines up to $7,500 or more, free annual fees for life and an array of discounts, points, coupons and credits on future purchases. One card issued by an airline even offered a coupon for a free round-trip companion ticket anywhere the airline flies in the United States when the customer signed up for its credit card.

The bargain cards often turn out to be more illusion than reality. Many card issuers who seek to steal from their competitors evaluate a consumer's credit history so finely that they reject about half the applications.

Unless you live under a rock, you're probably aware that some of America's biggest nonbank companies, such as AT&T, General Motors, Ford and General Electric, are elbowing one another for a piece of the credit card business. The reason, as Willie Sutton once said about banks, is that's where the money is, and that's where the profits are. Credit card issuers make after-tax profits of about $3.5 billion a year. In 1987, nonbank cards accounted for only about 20 percent of the business; today, it's almost 50 percent and growing fast.

With this kind of money pouring onto the bottom line, department stores, gasoline companies, supermarkets and other retailers want a bigger piece of the action. They are rushing to join the banks and big corporations with their own plastic Visa or Master-Cards. Kroger, the big Cincinnati-based grocery chain, will offer MasterCards to its customers, and Nordstrom, the Seattle-based department store chain, will issue its own Visa card. Shell Oil Company wants to make your gasoline credit card a MasterCard. Not only will you be able to buy gas, but you can shop till you drop at the local department store. "The only credit card you'll need," says Shell.

Within the credit card industry, the retailer cards are referred to as *cobranded cards*. Because retailers are interested in attracting customers to their own stores, the cobranded cards are expected to be more competitive than typical bank cards. Kroger, for example, promises its MasterCard holders an annual 1 to 2 percent rebate, interest rates half of what many bank cards charge and no annual fees. Shell will allow drivers to save money at the pump and receive rebates on other purchases.

Credit card companies also offer a credit protection plan, and you are guaranteed enrollment. The plan pays the minimum monthly amount due on your credit card bill if you are unable to work because of involuntary unemployment, illness or accident. The payments continue for up to one full year or until you go back to work, whichever comes first. In the event of death, the plan will pay off the entire card balance up to $5,000. That may sound like a good idea until you look at the cost—an extra 2 percent a month based on your outstanding card balance. This is very expensive disability and life insurance protection, which you can avoid with adequate insurance policies.

Credit Card Profits

Credit card companies don't make a profit on what you buy; they make a profit on what you don't pay back each month. Just how profitable is it for the likes of GM, Ford, Citibank and now retailers such as Kroger, Shell and Nordstrom to keep you on the hook for hefty interest charges?

Let's say you run up a $2,000 balance on your credit card. (The average cardholder, who regularly carries a monthly balance, has a debt of $3,300 spread over roughly six credit cards.) Now let's say you decide not to charge on the card again until you pay off the balance. The minimum monthly payment, around 2 percent of the balance, is about $40 a month. Of that amount, $33.13 will go for interest expense on a card with a 19.8 percent rate, and only $6.67 to reduce your outstanding balance. At the end of the first year, if you send in only the minimum amount required each month, your $2,000 debt will be reduced by just $100! The card issuers are feeding at the trough, while the cardholders are on a crash diet.

It gets even worse. If you continue to send in the minimum amount each month and don't make any more charges, you'll be paying off the original $2,000 debt for the next 31 years! By the time you make the final payment, it will have cost you $7,126 to pay off a $2,000 balance. When most people realize how credit card interest payments can send their financial security up in flames, they often visualize the bank manager who issued the card standing there holding the matchbook and gasoline can—grinning.

Your credit card company loves you, and why not. Gerri Detweiler, executive director of Bankcard Holders of America (BHA), a nonprofit organization that educates bankcard holders, says,

"To paraphrase Ross Perot, that big sucking sound you hear is your money draining from your wallet to your banker's bottom line." The whole idea of offering credit cards with fancy extras is to persuade more consumers to keep high monthly balances on the books for as long as possible. In order to make it even easier for you to run up more debt—and pay more interest—credit card issuers have reduced the required minimum monthly payments. One credit card company now has a minimum monthly payment as low as 1.67 percent of the monthly balance on its gold card. Some issuers will even let you skip a payment. Why is this important?

First, according to the credit card industry, 43 percent of consumers sometimes or always make minimum payments on their credit cards. Second, the lower the minimum monthly payment, the greater the profit to the card issuer. Again, using our $2,000 balance and minimum monthly payments, if you can boost your repayments from $40 a month to $70 a month, you will cut the repayment schedule in our example from 31 years to just 39 months! On the other hand, if you add as little as 25 cents a day, $7.50 a month, to your monthly payment, you can save as much as $5,000 in interest! You'll move a big chunk of the bank's bottom line to your own simply by paying an extra two bits a day.

If you pay more than the required minimum, the next month the card issuer can reduce the minimum payment by the extra amount you paid that month. Many people make the minimum payment each month and don't realize that their outstanding balance may be going up, not down, because their payments are less than the finance charges.

Basic Rule #18:

Shop for a new credit card.

It should come as no surprise that people who pay off their balance in full each month get the best credit card deals. The banks and other credit card issuers hate these people, but they can make their money from the other 72 percent of consumers who typically carry a revolving card balance each month. That's up from only 50 percent in 1987. Here are some tips on looking for the best credit card.

For a "Payoff" Card

The key elements to look for in a card when you intend to pay the balance in full each month are:

- 25- to 30-day grace period. This gives you time to pay off the balance each month without incurring any interest. There are rich rewards for the nimble and courageous shopper, but only if you pay the *full* balance each month. If you underpay—even by $1—you can be charged interest on the full amount of the balance to the date of the statement. Most consumers don't realize that they can lose the grace period if they regularly revolve.
- Lowest annual fees. There is no reason why card issuers should charge you an annual fee. They earn a "merchant fee" of as much as 2.5 percent of the purchase amount every time you use the card. Many cards have eliminated their annual fees, but some card fees can still run as high as $40 a year. Some cards must be used at least six times a year to avoid the annual fee. Try to find one that charges no annual fees and issues additional cards to other family members without charge.
- Interest rates. If you intend to pay off the balance each month, you don't care what the interest rate is because you won't be incurring any interest. Some of the high-interest-rate cards offer the best deal to those who pay off the balance in full each month.

For a "Credit Balance" Card

The key element to look for in a card where you intend to carry a credit balance is a low interest rate. Most of the low-interest-rate cards today have a variable rate, usually the prime rate plus a set amount. A 15 percent card uses the prime rate (currently 6 percent) plus 9 percent. Like an adjustable-rate mortgage, the interest rate on your credit card balance can change as interest rates rise or fall.

While these variable rates can be as low as half the current rate of many fixed-rate cards, they often come with strings. For example, a new credit card offered a variable interest rate of 11.9 percent (prime of 6 percent plus 5.9 percent), but to get this low rate you had to pay interest charges from date of purchase. There was no grace period to pay off the statement in full each month, late fees were $15, over-the-limit fees were $15, and cash advance fees were as much as $20.

Methods of Interest Calculation

There are four basic ways that credit card companies can figure your outstanding balance. From best to worst, they are:

1. average daily balance, excluding new purchases
2. two-cycle average daily balance, excluding new purchases
3. average daily balance, including new purchases
4. two-cycle average daily balance, including new purchases

Most card issuers figure interest charges on a one-month period. The amount outstanding each day is totaled and divided by the number of days in the month to get the average daily balance.

Here's how the two-cycle method works, according to Robert McKinley of RAM Research: "Say your previous balance was zero and you charge a $1,000 purchase on January 1. When your January statement arrives in February, you can either pay the balance off in full, thus avoiding interest charges, or make a partial payment and incur interest. If you decide to pay less than the full balance, you will be assessed interest (on your February statement) from January 1. Under the one-cycle method, card issuers assess interest only for February." The two-cycle method can be quite deceiving, so consider this: Theoretically, a cardholder paying off the full balance every third month could incur up to four extra months of interest per year.

The card issuer can make substantially more interest income on the same credit card debt depending on the way interest is calculated. Here's an example of a shopper who charged $1,000 the first month, paid the minimum amount due, charged another $1,000 the next month, and paid the entire balance. The cardholder repeated this pattern three more times during the year.

Interest Rate	*12%*	*17.3%*	*19.8%*
Average daily balance, excluding new purchases	$ 40.00	$ 57.60	$ 66.00
Average daily balance, including new purchases	80.00	115.20	132.00
Two-cycle average daily balance, including new purchases	120.00	172.80	198.00

SOURCE: Reprinted by permission of Bankcard Holders of America.

If you carry a balance and pay interest each month, the card issuers are making a clever gamble that you'll believe the low interest rate in the advertisements and not the actual rate you pay. Here is a list of the sneaky tricks card issuers use to boost your interest expense on outstanding balances.

- Sneaky Trick #1: Teaser rates. To attract new customers, some card issuers offer a lower interest rate for a certain period. The idea is that if you once make the move to a new card, sharply higher interest rates won't later induce you to find a lower-rate card.
- Sneaky Trick #2: Start the interest clock now. A growing number of credit cards start charging interest on credit balances the date you make the purchases—in most cases, even before you leave the store.
- Sneaky Trick #3: Compounding interest. Some card issuers now use daily compounding of interest instead of monthly compounding. This means that interest is calculated and added to your balance daily instead of monthly.
- Sneaky Trick #4: Time-tiered rates. Some card issuers have introduced an interest rate gimmick called a *time-tiered rate*. Current purchases, including those made in the previous month, are charged a lower rate, while purchases that are more than two

billing cycles old are charged a much higher rate. A recent ad for a new credit card highlighted the low rate of 9.9 percent. In the fine print, however, came this message: "The rate is 9.9 percent on current and prior month purchases. Purchases more than two months old will carry a 15.9 percent rate." Those who carry a credit balance for any length of time under the time-tiered method of calculating interest used in this example will find that most of their actual interest costs are not at the headline-grabbing 9.9 percent, but at almost 16 percent.

How To Reduce Credit Card Debt

Of course, the best way to cut your credit card debt is what I suggested at the beginning of this chapter—simply cancel your cards. If you can't wean yourself altogether, at least reduce the number of cards you carry to one or two. Following are a few suggestions to help you use your cards wisely.

- Charge only what you can repay at month's end. People often ask me how to boost their 3 or 4 percent savings account yield at the bank, yet these same people are often paying 17 or 18 percent interest on their credit card debt. That's a 14 percent *loss* in managing their money. The farmers who paid cash for day-to-day expenses would never think of doing that.

   Another point to consider is that credit card debt is no longer tax-deductible. If you are in a 28 percent federal tax bracket, you would need to find an investment paying 26 percent before taxes just to cover the 18 percent interest expense.

- Pay off revolving charge card balances as soon as possible. If you can, take some of your low-yielding savings and pay off your credit card debt now. Or, if you've paid off a department store card on which you were paying $50 a month, apply that $50 to another credit card balance. Do that until you pay off all your credit cards. If you can't make these payments, use some of the money you pay yourself first before you invest.

   BHA offers a program called "Debt Zapper" that shows card-holders how to pay off their credit cards in the fastest, least expensive way possible. For $10, you'll get a personalized report that shows you exactly how much to pay on each card each month until they're all paid off. To order, call 703-481-1110.

- Don't use your credit cards for cash advances. Most cards charge interest immediately on cash advances and also slap on a hefty fee for the privilege. For example, a cash advance of $300 with an average fee of only $2.50, plus interest at 18.5 percent from the date of the cash advance, will have an effective interest rate of about 33 percent even if you pay back the monthly statement in full at the end of the month.

- Pay promptly. Send in your payment as soon as you receive the monthly statement, even if you don't pay the full balance. That's important because many card issuers use the average daily balance method for computing interest charges. Under this method, the interest clock is ticking each day. Over the long run, this can make a big difference in the actual interest expense you incur. Most cards also assess an average late payment fee of $15 if your check arrives at the credit card company beyond the cutoff date.

If You Lose Your Credit Card

If your cards are lost or stolen, be sure to call the credit card issuers immediately. Most credit card companies have a 24-hour hot line number for reporting missing cards. Once you report the missing cards, the law says you have no further liability, and your maximum out-of-pocket liability is $50 per card for unauthorized charges. Most card issuers can give you a new number in minutes. It is a good idea to follow up your phone call with a letter to the credit card company sent by certified mail.

Credit card fraud is on the increase. For the four major credit cards—Visa, MasterCard, Discover and Optima—the losses in the United States due to fraud rose from only $125 million in 1983 to $720 million in 1992. Although you may not be financially responsible for the unauthorized use of your credit card, a few precautions when you use your card can avoid the inconvenience of straightening out your account later.

- Keep your credit cards concealed. If you leave them out in the open, scam operators can copy the numbers and use your card. Telephone credit cards are particularly sought by thieves who then sell your card number to people who use it to make long-distance calls around the world.
- Keep the carbon copies from purchase charges and cash advances. A carbon copy of your receipt is as good as the credit card itself to a crook.
- Do not give out your credit card number and expiration date over the phone to someone you don't know or to someone who is offering free trips or prizes if you first show "good faith" by making a payment.
- Destroy all cards you no longer use. If you get a renewal card, it will probably carry the same number as your old one.

How To Find the Best Deal in a Credit Card

The good news, if you already have a hefty balance on your card and can't pay it off any time soon, is that card issuers have discovered that almost everyone who wants a credit card already has one. To pry customers from their competitors, most card issuers offer a balance transfer program in which they will help you roll over your current debt to the new card. In many cases, the new card will offer a lower interest rate on the transferred balance just to get you to switch.

A credit card debt rollover is similar to an IRA rollover. The new card issuer may give you checks on your new account to pay off your old debt, and in some cases, the card issuer will make the transfer of debt for you.

There are two good sources for finding the best credit card:

- Bankcard Holders of America (560 Herndon Pkwy., Suite 120, Herndon, VA 22070, offers a list of low-interest credit cards with information to help you find the best card for your situation for $4. They also have a booklet, *Your Credit Rights: Rebuilding Credit and Getting out of Debt*. Call them at 703-481-1110.)

- RAM Research has monitored credit cards since 1986. They track credit card fees and interest rates and publish a monthly *CardTrak* newsletter that lists hundreds of current credit cards, information on how to find the best one and background stories on the latest credit card offerings. Cost is $5 a copy. (RAM Research, Box 1700, Frederick, MD 21702, 800-344-7714.)

If You Can't Get a Credit Card

If you have a bad credit history and are now working your way out of debt, or if you have insufficient credit history, the major credit card issuers may turn down your application for a new card. A great way to rebuild your credit and flash a Visa or MasterCard as you do, is to obtain a *secured* credit card. Even if your credit history shows liens, charge-offs, repossessions or bankruptcy, as long as your problems are under control and in the past, you are likely to qualify for a secured credit card.

To obtain a secured credit card you have to establish a savings account with the bank. If you don't pay your bills, the bank can use the money in the savings account to meet the payments. For example, the minimum savings deposit can range from $500 to $2,500 depending on what credit line you want. Depending on the issuer and your credit history, the credit line can vary from 50 percent to 150 percent of your deposit. Most issuers of secured credit cards will pay interest on your savings account, but some pay only the passbook savings rate. Most secured cards charge higher interest rates and higher annual fees than unsecured cards, and a one-time application fee is often charged.

A secured Visa or MasterCard looks and works just like any other credit card. It is simply a bank credit card guaranteed by a savings deposit.

If you want to apply for a secured credit card, deal only with a bank. Don't fall for the newspaper and magazine ads that guarantee to find you a credit card, no matter what your credit history, for an advance payment of $150 or more. You can do the job better yourself.

Key Federal Savings Bank, the nation's most established secured card issuer, has a free booklet, *Managing Your Credit, What You Should Know About Secured Cards*. To order, call 800-228-5757. Both RAM Research and Bankcard Holders of America have a list of secured credit card programs.

CHAPTER 7

Protecting Yourself and Your Family

"When you write your book," Bill Thomas told me at a workshop, as he sat in his motorized wheelchair, "be sure to tell the readers what I didn't do. I spent too much money on things I didn't need and almost none on what I really needed—protection from catastrophic loss." He looked at me with deep hurt in his eyes. "I've lost my job, my home, my wife, my self-respect. Tell them that disability is a living death."

In order to protect all that you've worked for, you need to protect yourself from the two major risks everyone runs: loss of life and loss of income. All the financial planning in the world won't cover these losses if you don't make adequate self-protection plans.

The purpose of this chapter is not to sell you insurance or to suggest that you avoid an insurance salesperson, but to help you understand the basics and how to plan for them.

Basic Rule #19:

**Buy insurance for catastrophic dollar
losses, not for temporary inconvenience.**

Insurance should provide a guaranteed monthly income if you become disabled and can't work. In the event of your death, it should provide adequate income for your family and pay off your major debts. These are risks most people can't afford to assume during their working life. On the other hand, protection against the loss of your credit cards or someone smashing the trunk of your car or your being abducted by aliens from a UFO is not essential. You can also forget about the expensive extra coverage of decreasing-term mortgage insurance or credit insurance. Instead, concentrate on two basic risks: disability and death protection.

Now let's get down to the basics of planning for the future.

Disability Insurance

If you acquire no other protection than life insurance, you need to buy disability insurance. From talking to countless people like Bill Thomas, I believe disability can indeed be a "living death." The sudden loss of income is often followed by a psychological depression when extra demands of family members are added to anxiety of worrying about what may lie ahead. The breadwinner faces the skyrocketing costs of medical expenses, nursing, rehabilitation and recuperation at the same time his or her ability to earn an income is lost. Statistics don't lie: According to the insurance industry, you are five times more likely to be disabled than to die during your working life.

Most people give little thought to how they would replace their income if they could not work. According to the Life Insurance Marketing and Research Association, only 18 percent of workers in the United States have any long-term disability insurance, even though disability claims are on the rise. Doctors today are saving the lives of many more patients who would have died a few years ago, but many of them won't be able to go back to work for years, if ever.

Many people think they have adequate disability coverage through their employer. For the most part, they don't. Benefits may continue for five years or less, and the group carriers are increasingly finding that people aren't disabled according to strictly enforced definitions in the policy.

Before you buy a disability policy or review the one you already have, it's important to understand the major factors that make up the policy.

Waiting Period

The waiting period, sometimes called the elimination period, is the time you will have to wait after you are disabled before the policy will pay benefits. Waiting periods vary from one month to one year, but most individual policies have a 90-day period, which means you'll receive your first check about 120 days after actually becoming disabled. Like auto policies where the collision damage premium is reduced as the deductible goes up, with disability policies, the longer the waiting period, the lower the premium. A good rule of thumb is that a 90-day waiting period will reduce the premium by about half as compared to a 30-day period, and a 180-day waiting period will reduce the premium by half as compared to a policy with a 90-day waiting period.

Term of Benefits

Many employer group policies pay benefits for only five years, or less. Some individual policies pay benefits to age 65 for sickness, and for life in the case of accident. The longer the insurer is on the hook to pay benefits, the more the policy will cost.

Monthly Income

An important factor to look at in a disability policy is the amount of your current monthly income it will replace. Most insurers limit their risk of replacement income to around 50 to 60 percent of your regular income.

Integration

This is a fancy word for the practice of reducing the disability policy's stated benefits because of other income or benefits you may receive when you become disabled. Insurers argue that they are only protecting you for the amount shown in the policy, and other benefits you may receive can be used to reduce their payouts. For example, assume that your regular income is $3,000 a month and that the coverage provided by your group disability policy will be $1,500 a month after the waiting period. Once disabled, however, you find that you can collect $500 a month from your state's workers' compensation plan for a short period and $1,000 a month from Social Security after a six-month waiting period. Your employer might also pay some continuing income or a bonus. Depending upon the policy's provisions, often concealed in the fine print, all or most of this income might be used to reduce the benefits payable under the policy. Let's suppose that the policy has a 50 percent integration level. Then, if you are receiving $1,000 a month of other income, $500 of that money could be used to reduce the insurer's payout, leaving a benefit of not $1,500, as shown in the policy, but $1,000 a month.

Continuing To Work

Many disability policies won't pay if you return to work or, in some cases, if you work more than a few hours a week. If you are back on the job, the insurer may claim that benefits need not be paid. The trick is not to throw out your claim, but to start the waiting period all over again. To overcome this problem, it's a good idea to include two important riders in your individual policy.

- Residual disability. If you can go back to work but at a much lower-paying or part-time job, this rider kicks in and assures payment of the difference between what you earn and what you'd collect if you were totally disabled under the policy. This is one rider that's worth the price.
- Own occupation. Known as "Your Own Occ" in the trade, this rider is important for higher earners or professionals. It assures you that the policy will continue to pay benefits even if you do go back to work. Loss of benefits occurs only if you can engage in the profession or trade for which you were trained.

Cost-of-Living Adjustments

Many insurers will allow you to increase your premiums each year, based on the consumer price index, so your monthly benefits will keep pace with inflation. You can forgo this option, but you can't go back and pick it up later. My advice is to take it. It's not expensive, and it's well worth the price. Another option is a rider that will boost your disability income relative to inflation after you begin collecting benefits. You can select a flat rate or a percentage of your benefits. This rider can be expensive, and it's not on my "must" list.

How To Buy a Disability Policy

In one word: carefully. There are two types of insurers in this business: those that are in business to collect premiums and those that are in business to pay claims. Most disability insurance sold today, including group employer benefit plans, are sold to collect premiums because the insurers believe that a claim is unlikely, and most of the time this is true. This saves the insurance company a lot of money and keeps the price of these policies as low as possible. Only when a claim is filed will the carrier begin the underwriting process and determine if the claim can or must be paid. These policies are easy to obtain. Often you just sign your name or fill out a short form and agree to pay the premiums. However, the wretched performance of claims payments under these easy-to-get policies filled with fine print should make you think twice before you put your financial security in their hands.

The other type of policy is underwritten from the start. As you are required to do when you apply for a life insurance policy, you may be required to take a medical exam, provide your medical history, give evidence of your income and agree to let the insurer take a peek at your driving record and other personal history. These policies can be difficult to buy because the insurer may be locking in a guarantee to pay out a sum that could exceed a life insurance contract. For example, say a person age 45 buys a $2,000 a month policy payable to age 65. If the claim were to start immediately, the carrier could be on the hook for almost half a million dollars!

The bottom line is this: There is no free lunch when it comes to protecting your income in case of an accident or illness. If you want disability coverage, avoid wasting money on easy-to-get policies that deny claims for the flimsiest of reasons, and don't depend on your employer group disability policy because you may change jobs and go uncovered. Instead, buy a fully underwritten individual policy from an insurer that specializes in this risk, fill out the application carefully, stating all the details of your medical history (a common reason insurers give for denying a claim is that the applicant lied or omitted information on the application), take a medical exam and a blood test, and pay the premium. Once the policy is issued, it can't be canceled unless the policyholder fails to pay the premium.

Basic Rule #20:

Don't skimp on your life insurance protection.

If 1,000 people chip in $10 each and one person dies during the year, the death benefit could be $10,000. No one knows in advance, of course, who will die during the year but, at the cost of a ten dollar bill, you have eliminated a risk at a very slight cost. But what if ten people died during the year? Now you need an insurance company that can insure hundreds of thousands of people and spread the risk so that a $10 payment can still provide a $10,000 death benefit. That's why life insurance is the business of taking a risk on death.

Since life insurance death benefits were likely to be paid to widows and orphans who needed every dollar they could collect, Congress long ago gave life insurance companies special privileges under the tax code. One privilege is that death benefits paid by life insurance companies are received income tax-free by the beneficiaries. The money you use to pay life insurance premiums is normally—but not always—taxable.

How Much Life Insurance Do You Need?

Single people may not need much life insurance protection, while a wage earner with four children may need a great deal. Chances are that you need a lot more life insurance than you think you do when you consider your loss of income along with the inflationary times that lie ahead. What you insure when you buy life insurance is your liabilities, not your assets. You should plan to cover your mortgage, current debts, college education for the kids and, most important of all, an adequate monthly income for your spouse and family.

You should first determine the death benefit you need without looking at the cost. The reason for buying life insurance in the first place is to provide instant financial protection in the event of the policyholder's death. A hefty savings plan won't do much good if what you really need is life insurance protection.

Buy a whole life policy with a savings plan only after you have covered the financial needs of those dependent on your continued income.

Most people who have future liabilities to cover buy too little life insurance because they think they can't afford more coverage. You may have to shop till you drop, but you can find life insurance protection at a cost that will surprise you and not devastate your pocketbook.

Any male under age 30, as a preferred nonsmoker risk in good health, can buy ten-year level-premium term insurance for as little as 80 cents per thousand dollars worth of insurance, per year. Females of the same age can purchase the same coverage for only about 63 cents. A $250,000 term life insurance policy for a male age 30 would cost about $250, a female about $207, including the annual policy fee, each year for the next ten years. At age 40, this same policy would cost a male about $375 per year, $250 for a female, and at age 50, a policy for a male would cost about $625 per year, a female $530. Females currently have a four-year setback, so in our example females age 40 pay about the same premium as males age 36.

If you smoke, however, the annual premiums climb like a tobacco truck going up Pike's Peak. The smoker's annual premium for $250,000 of insurance is $502 for a 30-year-old male and $362 for a female. At age 40, it's $905 for a male and $545 for a female. And at age 50, it's $1,845 for a male and $1,017 for a female.

Another big mistake people often make is to buy the wrong kind of coverage for their needs. As a result, life insurance is often sold to people for the wrong reason. Statistics bear this out. There was a time, before IRAs and 401(k) plans, when people bought a whole life insurance policy and kept it in force until their death or retirement. It offered a guaranteed way to protect the family in the event of the breadwinner's early death, and it forced people to save for retirement later on. Today, according to the life insurance industry, half of all term policies lapse by the end of the fourth year, and half of all cash value (permanent) policies by the end of the ninth year.

Only 3 percent of policyholders keep their permanent policies in force for 20 years.

Based on these industry figures, policies sold to provide retirement income are, in reality, a side trip to the financial poorhouse. "Lapse rates are so high that the turnover is astonishing," says an executive of a life insurance company. "What's worse," he says, "the consumers who keep their policies have to subsidize those who jump out early."

Part of the blame for lapsed policies belongs at the door of the insurance industry. In an effort to sell more insurance, many companies price their new policies for persons of the same age and risk lower than those that are already on the books. Part of the reason is that the cost of insuring an individual has declined. In the 1920s, the mortality rate in America was 1,300 people per 100,000 of population. Today, it's slightly over 800 people per 100,000. The cost of reinsuring the risk has also declined sharply. For these reasons, new policy premiums are often as much as 30 to 40 percent lower than for existing policies. A policyholder looks at the premium for the fifth year of his current policy and compares that to the lower premiums for a new policy offered by a competing agent. It becomes apparent that, if he's in good health, he can save a lot of money by trading in the old policy and buying a new one.

Moving Your Policy to Another Insurer

If you find yourself with an insurer you believe is financially weak and may be taken over by the state insurance regulators (see Chapter 11 for ways to check out the financial condition of insurance companies), you can move your policy to another insurer and avoid any tax liability. This can be handled by your new insurer. If you are transferring a whole life policy, you may have to requalify medically and pass other requirements of the new insurer. You may also have to pay a new "reduced" sales commission. If you are transferring a tax-deferred annuity without death benefits, the move should be made swiftly, but you may be stuck with a deferred sales commission when you cash out your policy to move it to another insurer.

Whole Life Insurance

The most frequently asked question about life insurance is: Should I buy term or whole life? The Guardian Insurance Company's recent study found that a whole life policy is a better buy if you keep it in force for at least ten years. For a $200,000 whole life policy on a male age 35, the annual premium is $2,786. Keeping the policy in force for 30 years, to age 65, the Guardian study reported an $86,705 advantage over a person who bought term and invested the difference.

What the study did not address is that a 35-year-old male with a growing family often needs death protection more than long-term retirement savings. While the whole life annual premium for the $200,000 policy is $2,786, the 15-year level term premium for the same amount of coverage for a nonsmoker is only about $398. The cash value buildup of whole life policies, so often illustrated with glowing numbers that promise wealth at retirement, can be an illusion. First, the higher the cash values and the surrender values, the easier the policies are to sell. By the 20th and 25th year, the values are positively eye-catching, yet they come at a low cost to the insurer because very few policyholders keep their policies in force that long to collect. Today, many of the illustrations of future cash values that spin out of the insurer's computers are only guesswork, based on various interest rate assumptions and mortality charges. To make the policies appear more competitive, the interest rate assumptions are often higher than the issuer is likely to pay in the future and, in many cases, higher than current policies now pay. For example, one insurer might assume a 10 percent annual rate of return in its computer-generated illustrations, another company might assume only an 8 percent return. The bottom line is this: An illustration is not a guarantee, or sometimes not even a best guess, of how the policy is going to look in 20 years or at age 65.

How do the insurance companies get away with these make-believe numbers? At the bottom of the illustration of what your policy is supposed to amount to in future years, you'll probably find a note that says something like: "This is an illustration, not a contract."

If you think the interest rate assumptions are too high, ask the agent for an illustration using lower rates. The figures you want to check before you buy a whole life policy are the *guaranteed* cash values and surrender values, the amount the insurance company is obligated to pay if you terminate the policy.

The second way in which the insurance company's cash value projections can be misleading is that the nest egg at retirement is contingent upon paying the annual premiums to age 65. To give buyers a better deal, some permanent policies have so-called "vanishing premiums." Such a policy assumes that the dividends in, say, the first ten years will be large enough to eliminate annual premiums thereafter. If the optimistic assumptions of dividend growth turn out to be less than enough to pay the premiums, the policyholder must pay the difference.

Third, at the death of the policyholder, the cash values can be used by the insurer to help pay the death claim and may not be returned to the beneficiary. (You can purchase a cash value rider on most permanent policies that will, in effect, insure the cash values at death.)

Universal Life Insurance

In the 1980s, with big money to be made in the stock market and other investments, the old-fashioned, low-yielding, whole life policy faced a grim future for the best prospects: the middle-aged family man. The idea was to spice up whole life in a new permanent policy called universal life. In response, insurance companies dumped the guaranteed premiums and cash values that often came with whole life in return for competitive earnings in higher-yielding investments. The concept is simple: Every premium you make goes into an account that earns interest or makes a profit from the investments. The insurer first deducts the money to pay for the pure death protection in the policy, called a *mortality charge,* then deducts administration and selling costs. The rest is your cash value buildup. Universal policies have two different commission charges. They may be *front-loaded,* where you pay the hefty sales commissions when you buy the policy, or *back-loaded,* where you pay the commissions on the entire amount in your account as surrender charges if you cash in the policy. Most insurers have moved to back-end loads to defer their selling expenses and make the accumulations in the policies appear more attractive.

In fact, universal life is an admission by the insurers that you can often do better buying term life insurance and investing the difference. In this case, however, the insurer does the job for you. You get the tax deferral of earnings inside the policy, but often the term premiums in universal life policies are greater than you would have to pay if you bought the policy yourself. Also, in some policies, if you cash out in the first year, you can lose almost the entire balance in your accumulation fund; in year two, as much as 75 percent; in year three, 50 to 60 percent. These surrender charges may be less in some policies, and in most cases they disappear by the fifth year or later.

Variable Life

Variable life policies are a cross between an IRA and a life insurance policy. They enable policyholders to invest in stock and bond mutual funds of their choice inside the policy where the assets grow tax-deferred until the money is withdrawn or is passed on tax-free to the beneficiary as life insurance death benefits.

The policyholder assumes a considerable risk for all these advantages. If your stock or bond investments go down in value, you may have to ante up some additional money to keep the life insurance policy in force as issued. If the return on your investments fails to pay for the coverage, your death benefit can fall. On the other hand, if your investments do well, your death benefit can increase.

Variable life policies also are the most expensive type of life insurance you can buy. They often have high expense ratios to cover the death benefit, the cost of buying and selling funds, and the insurer's administration and selling costs. Variable life policies are also long-term buys. In the first year, the cost of termination, sometimes called *surrender penalties,* can run to half the money you originally invested. The termination charges usually decline over the first five or ten years.

Variable life policies are often bought because they delay income taxes on the buildup of assets in the policy. Nonetheless, variable life policies make sense only if you have a limited need for death protection, plan to hold the policy for at least 20 years or want to pass on the assets to your heirs in the event of your death.

Guaranteed-Issue Life Insurance

Many insurers offer life insurance without a medical examination. The policies have guaranteed premiums, cash values and death benefits. The typical policy is issued between the ages of 55 and 80 with a maximum death benefit of $25,000. However, because the policy is issued without medical information, if death occurs from illness within three years of policy issue for ages 55 to 64, or two years for ages 65 to 80, typically the company will return only the premiums paid plus 5 percent interest. If death occurs from an accident at any age, the company will not only pay the full death benefit in the policy, but also the premiums paid plus 5 percent interest.

Borrowing from a Whole Life Policy

In most cases, your policy loan limit is based on your guaranteed surrender cash value. You may generally borrow up to 90 percent of the guaranteed cash value and still keep the policy in force, but you don't get something for nothing. Buried in the fine print is this message: "The amount of your outstanding loan, and unpaid interest charges if any, will be deducted from the death benefit that is payable to the beneficiaries."

One of the selling points for whole life insurance in previous years was that you could borrow from your whole life policy at 3 or 4 percent interest rates to help pay the premiums. Known as *minimum deposit,* it was a handy way to reduce your net cash outlay and, in some cases, let the expected dividends pay part or all of the interest charges and premiums.

Today, insurers charge current market interest rates, around 7 or 8 percent, and the interest paid on the policy loans is no longer tax-deductible.

Term Life Insurance

A term policy is like "renting" the coverage, similar to auto and fire insurance. Your annual premium covers only that year's death protection. A term policy typically has no cash value and pays no dividends.

Term life is sold with level premiums for one year, called *annual renewable term* (ART), and renewable to age 90. Other term policies have guaranteed level premiums for 5, 10, 15 and even 20 years. At the end of these periods, the life insurance is renewable at sharply higher premium levels, based on the policyholder's current age.

Another form of term insurance is *decreasing term,* in which the annual premium remains the same but the death benefit declines. These term policies are most often sold to pay off the mortgage on the theory that, while the death benefit declines each year, so does the loan balance.

Reentry Provisions

Some term policies have reentry provisions that allow for lower premiums if the you pass a physical exam every five years, or when you reach a certain age. The insurer can't cancel the policy if you don't take advantage of this option, or fail to qualify, but premiums can rise drastically. For example, on a $100,000 term policy on a male age 43 who qualifies for reentry, the annual premium is about $468. If the insured can't qualify, the annual premium can rise to around $800. Be wary of "reentry" term policies that require you to pass a physical from time to time in order to continue paying the original premiums stated in the policy.

Waiver of Premium

Most term and whole life policies offer a waiver of premium rider that will pay the annual premiums if you are disabled and can't work. This is a good idea because the cost is low and the policy stays in force if you become disabled. If you allow the policy to lapse from nonpayment of premiums when you are disabled, you may not be able to purchase any new life insurance in the future.

Conversion

Many life insurance companies will allow a term policy to be converted into a whole life policy without a medical exam. Called *guaranteed conversion,* this option allows the insured to convert from rising-premium term insurance to fixed-premium whole life. In order to entice more term policyholders to convert to higher premium whole life, many insurers offer incentives such as a give-back of the last year's term premium, which can then be applied to the first year's whole life premium. Most insurers will not allow a whole life policy to be converted into a term policy.

By now you've probably concluded that the purchase of life insurance means making a commitment to a sizable investment each year over the next 20 or 30 years. Your best protection is to find the most qualified agent you can, preferably one with a Certified Life Underwriter (CLU) designation, with at least five years in the business, who represents several life insurance companies. Then you'll want to ask all the what-if questions. What if the projections you show don't pan out? What if I have to cash out the policy early? What if the accumulations in the illustration are not guaranteed?

What if the annual premium takes off like a rocket and my budget remains fixed at the old level?

How To Select a Life Insurance Policy

Your first decision in shopping for life insurance is to determine what you want the policy to do. If you want a savings plan with death benefits, then whole life or universal life will probably be your choice. If you want low-cost death protection only, then you'll want to consider term insurance.

The following chart compares a typical $250,000 whole life insurance policy for a male, nonsmoker, age 45, and a 15-year level term policy. Actual premiums will vary by insurer, and they may be more or less than shown.

Year	Age	Whole Life Premium	Cash Surrender Value	Term Premium	Cash Value
1	45	$ 4,558	$ 00	$ 975	$00
2	46	4,558	2,952	975	00
3	47	4,558	7,663	975	00
4	48	4,558	12,671	975	00
5	49	4,558	17,985	975	00
End of 5 years		22,790	17,985	4,875	00
End of 10 years		45,558	51,115	9,750	00
End of 15 years		68,370	96,982	14,625	00

Your choices are either to let the insurance company invest your excess premiums over the cost of the insurance and keep the whole life's annual premium level as long as you keep the policy in force or to buy pure death protection with an increasing premium. In this example, the term premium after 15 years, at age 60, rises from $975 a year to around $2,500 a year, while the whole life premium remains the same, and the cash values continue to build.

Your net cost over 15 years with whole life is a gain of $28,612 (the cash surrender value of $96,982 less your premiums of $68,370). Your net cost will continue to decline as long as you keep the whole life policy in force and pay the premiums. The net cost of the term policy is $14,625, but the annual premiums will rise sharply during the next 15-year period. To get the true cost during this period, you must take into consideration the interest income or profits you could have earned had you invested the difference between the whole life premium and the term premium each year. If you have the willpower to invest the difference in a stock mutual fund, based on the past 20 years' performance, you'd have a greater net value than most whole life policies.

The success of whole life has been based on the fact that most people don't invest the difference, and so it is sometimes referred to as *forced savings*. The other advantage of whole life, as with an IRA, is that taxes on the cash value buildup are deferred until you withdraw the money. If you choose a term policy and invest the difference, the income you earn is taxable each year unless you put the investment in a tax-qualified retirement plan.

Premiums

The premiums you pay for life insurance are affected by several factors: your age, your health, whether or not you smoke and other aspects of your personal life. Here's how these factors can affect the annual premium for a $100,000 ten-year level-premium term policy with a $60 annual policy fee:

Age	PNS	NS	SK
35, male	$ 151	$ 202	$ 365
35, female	134	175	300
45, male	254	367	730
45, female	204	293	552
55, male	518	760	1,460
55, female	348	501	970
65, male	1,250	1,775	3,330
65, female	763	1,068	2,064

PNS = Preferred nonsmoker
NS = Standard nonsmoker
SK = Smoker

A typical preferred nonsmoker (PNS) rate would include the following requirements:

The individuals must not have smoked cigarettes, pipes or cigars or used any form of smokeless tobacco within the last 12 months. After remaining tobacco-free for 12 months, former tobacco users may qualify for nontobacco rates on their next anniversary, subject to evidence. The applicant must be in excellent health with a cholesterol/HDL ratio 5.5 or less, no history of alcohol or drug abuse for seven years, blood pressure less than 140/90 and no parent or sibling with coronary artery disease or cerebrovascular disease prior to the age of 60. The individual must also have a clean driving record and not engage in hazardous activities, such as skydiving, flying airplanes, bungee jumping or motor sports.

The nonsmoker standard rate (NS) is for individuals who don't smoke, are in good health and otherwise qualify for a policy.

The smoker rate (SK) is for individuals who smoke tobacco, are in good health and otherwise qualify for the policy.

There is also a substandard rating system for individuals who have a history of medical problems. The most common conditions that result in "rated" policies are diabetes, substance abuse, hazardous avocation, obesity, hypertension, coronary artery disease and cancer. Depending on the health risk, the policy can be rated from A to G, or 1 to 16. The higher the rating, the more the standard premium is increased. The good news is that most people with a health problem can buy life insurance. The annual premiums may be two or three times above the standard rate, but the coverage is often a good investment for someone who needs the protection.

Medical Information Bureau

Ever wonder how the insurance companies learn about your risk of dying from a heart attack, how often you skydive, your driving habits and other personal information? It's easy. It takes about two minutes and costs about 25 cents to plug into the insurance industry's huge data bank at the Medical Information Bureau (MIB) near Boston. Most of the American and Canadian insurers use this database to help them underwrite your application for a health, life or disability policy.

The MIB's records may be updated every time you apply for insurance. A report is sent if the underwriter believes that the applicant's medical or background check indicates a higher-than-average risk or the potential for fraud. Because the watchdog group at the MIB is looking over your shoulder, it's a good idea to be completely honest about your medical and personal history when you apply for insurance.

To learn more about the MIB, write for their free booklet, *The Consumer's MIB Fact Sheet,* and for instructions on how to request a copy of your personal file. (MIB, Box 105, Essex Station, Boston, MA 02112. In Canada, MIB, 330 University Ave., Toronto, Canada M5G 1R7.)

Accelerated Death Benefits

The latest wrinkle in the life insurance industry is an accelerated death benefit (ADB) rider. With a growing number of people suffering from illnesses such as AIDS and cancer, more than 150 life insurers now allow policyholders to collect all or part of the death benefit early if they are terminally ill with less than 12 months to live. ADB provisions are sometimes included in new policies, and most life insurance companies offer them as a rider to existing policies. The American Council of Life Insurance expects the Internal Revenue Service to rule that, as with regular life insurance death benefits, these early payouts will also be received tax-free.

The National Insurance Consumer hot line (800-942-4242) will answer your questions and send you information on all aspects of disability and life insurance. The group is sponsored by the insurance industry.

Disability and life insurance are two of the most unusual purchases most individuals ever make. They require us to sacrifice our current lifestyle for a future event that might not happen. The payoff is a worry-free future for yourself and your loved ones and the knowledge that you have your priorities back on track.

CHAPTER 8

Delaying Taxes to Retirement

"We cannot know where we are going, any of us, until we know where we have been and where we now find ourselves."

Many people believe that the future can be told from the past. I happen to be one of them. In fact, this English proverb may be as relevant today as it was when Richard II nailed it to the wall of Winchester Church in 1386.

Evolution of Retirement Plans in America

The dawn of retirement plans in America broke across the landscape in 1875, when the Railway Express Company, later to become the American Express Company, established what is believed to be the first private pension plan. The idea of retirement was not new; what was new was the idea that income could be received in old age *without* work. "You can't understand the importance of retirement income," a factory worker wrote in 1896, "until you've seen a former worker starve for lack of the price of a meal."

It was now becoming clear to big business that urban industrial workers of the 1890s, without savings, were staying on the job until their last breath. In fact, as recently as 1900, almost 70 percent of all working men in the United States age 65 or over were still at work. Workers were holding onto their jobs and simply refusing to retire in acceptable numbers. The depression of the 1890s only exacerbated the problem.

As a result, the Railway Express pension plan and its later counterparts were established literally to force a growing number of older workers to retire. Retirement plans, it turned out, were good for business. The private pension plans established between 1875 and 1920 were a form of "pension arrangement." They were considered gratuities, not wages, and the business owners were free to pay the benefits or to turn them off at will. Workers had no rights in the plan, and none were ever intended.

The early pension plans established the following rules:

- They provided a defined benefit, based on salary, at age 65, usually a lifetime monthly income.
- The benefit was contingent upon working for the same employer for 25 to 30 years, without a break in service.
- The benefit was available only if the worker stayed on the job to age 65 or retired under the terms of the employer's pension plan.
- The employer was to make all the contributions to the plan.

By the 1980s, the philosophy had changed, and company-paid defined benefit pensions were in retreat for two reasons. First, rising inflation continued to push up salaries on which the retirement benefits are based, and companies were forced to feed a cash-hungry pension system to meet the ever-higher monthly retirement checks.

Second, people were living longer and, therefore, collecting more benefits in retirement. In 1946, life expectancy at age 65 was only 13.5 years. Today, it's about 18.5 years. On average, that's 60 more inflation-bloated monthly benefit checks per retiree than pension managers estimated just five decades earlier.

According to the Securities and Exchange Commission (SEC), some companies have minimized their obligations to retirees by assuming a higher-than-market interest rate to calculate their pension liability. A reduction of only 1 percent in the assumed rates of return can boost a company's pension liability by 10 percent, depending on the age of current workers and the benefits promised.

Back in 1950, when the Ford Motor Company started making pension payments, it had 62 active workers for each retiree. Today, that ratio is only 1.2 to 1—almost as many active workers as retirees. General Motors paid out $2.1 billion to cover 261,000 of its retirees and expects, by the end of 1994, to have a $19 billion shortfall in its pension plan to cover the pensions of its future retirees. Other companies, stuck with long-term pension plans, have more money going out in retirement checks than they are contributing for workers yet to retire. By any measure of dollar counting, the nation's current pension debt, and its promise to pay hefty retirement checks in later years to future retirees, has already become so great that it could put a severe drag on company profits. A company pension manager told me that he feels like an anvil salesman with his own merchandise in the trunk. No matter how many changes he makes, he still can't move the car.

As a result of these problems, added to vastly increased government regulations, the decline of company-paid pensions could be the biggest revolution in personal finance since the advent of mutual funds. Tens of thousands of American companies are eliminating their costly defined benefit pension plans and requiring workers to pay part of the bill. According to the Internal Revenue Service, American companies are eliminating their costly defined benefit pension plans in record numbers. Terminations soared more than 300 percent between the start of the 1980s and the end of the decade.

Already more workers are covered by retirement plans that require them to make contributions, or are not covered at all, than are in company-paid pension plans.

As this shift away from guaranteed pensions picks up speed and more and more companies bail out of costly plans, members of the baby boom generation will find company-paid pension plans have nearly vanished by the time they retire, replaced by plans that leave the workers responsible for paying part of the costs and managing their own investments.

What's Fair?

Over the years, Congress has unleashed a tidal wave of different plans, rules and tax laws that have most workers confused about how to save for retirement. What's even worse, the options that are available make a mockery of any attempt at fairness to all American workers. The cruel hoax is that those who don't understand the complex regulations have no reverse gear to use if they want to back up and start over after they've made a decision.

To get an idea of how disparate retirement plan benefits can be, consider this scenario: Four workers enter an elevator. One says, "I have a TSA 403(b) retirement plan at work, and I take a tax deduction right off the top of my salary for almost 20 percent of my pay. Then I boost that figure by making up for past years when I couldn't make contributions because we were raising the children."

"Not bad," says another worker. "I have a 401(k) plan where my employer matches my contributions dollar for dollar. With my company's help, I sock away about $12,000 a year, of which only half is my own money."

"I can top that," says another. "I'm self-employed, and I have a defined benefit retirement plan, so I take a tax deduction for over half my income."

The fourth worker looks at the floor as the elevator continues to rise. "My company has a profit-sharing plan," he says, "and with business so poor I'll be lucky if the company puts $500 into my plan by year's end. On top of that, I can't even make a tax-deductible contribution to my IRA."

Today, under our complex tax laws, the size of the annual deductible retirement plan contribution is based not on fairness, but on where an individual works and how much he or she knows about the various options that are available.

Basic Rule #21:

Don't rely on your company-paid pension.

Vesting

Millions of baby boomers who think they'll retire on company-paid retirement plans have overlooked the importance of vesting. Of all the fine print in the rules of your retirement plan, the vesting schedule may be the most important in reducing your future retirement income. Most books on financial planning don't even cover vesting, yet the lack of vesting is the single biggest reason why job-hopping workers fail to accumulate a retirement nest egg.

Vesting is one of the magic words in retirement plans. It tells you how much of the employer's contributions and earnings in a retirement plan you can take with you if you leave your job, get laid off or retire. All of your prior contributions, and the earnings, will be returned to you, but the vesting schedule in your plan will determine how much of the company's money you'll get to keep.

Here's how a typical company retirement plan, including the vesting schedule, might work:

1. You must become eligible to participate in the plan if you are at least 21 years old and on the job for at least one year.
2. Once you become eligible and join the plan, the company contributes money into your account each year, usually based on a percentage of salary or income. You can often make contributions yourself through voluntary payroll deductions.
3. When you are no longer employed by the company, the chances are that you will also be terminated from the company retirement plan. The amount of money contributed by the employer, plus the earnings in the account, will be paid to you based on the vesting schedule in your plan.

Currently, there are two main vesting schedules:

Gradual Vesting

No vesting for the first two years; then 20 percent after three years and 20 percent each year thereafter until the employee is 100 percent vested after seven years. For example, if the company's contributions were $1,000 a year and the account earned 10 percent a year:

Year of Service	Total Value of Account	Percentage Vested	Dollar Vested
1	$ 1,100	0%	$ 0
2	2,310	0	0
3	3,641	20	728
4	5,105	40	2,042
5	6,716	60	4,030
6	8,487	80	6,790
7	10,436	100	10,436

Instant Vesting

No vesting for as long as five years. After that, the employee must be 100 percent vested for all employer contributions and earned income made up to that time and thereafter, as long as the employee is on the job and covered under the retirement plan. If a worker leaves the company before the plan's fifth anniversary date, he or she could see all of the highly touted company contributions go up in smoke.

For More Information

Vesting schedules vary among employers, and some choose more rapid vesting. Typically, you are fully vested if you die or become totally and permanently disabled. In some cases, you may have to wait until retirement age to start collecting the benefits. If you are unsure of your vesting schedule or want to learn more about your company's retirement plan, ask your employer for a copy of the summary plan description booklet. It's also a good idea to get the free government booklet called "*Your Pension: Things You Should Know About Your Pension Plan.*" Write to: Pension Benefit Guaranty Corporation, 1200 K St., N.W., Washington, DC 20005-4026.

If you are having trouble collecting benefits, a great source I use is the nonprofit Pension Rights Center, 918 16th St., N.W., Suite 704, Washington, DC 20006, 202-296-3776. Its staff attorneys have helped countless individuals win pension benefits they were wrongly denied. They also offer a wide range of booklets on retirement plans and your pension rights at divorce.

Disbursement Options

Bruce Springsteen's ballad of the early 1980s now rings true: "They're closing down the textile mill across the railroad tracks. The foreman says these jobs are goin', boys, and they ain't coming back."

All across America, as the smokestack industries give way to services, the downsizing and restructuring of corporate jobs will continue. In fact, millions of workers today feel they are unsafe in any job. With the loss of the job, or with early retirement, the employer often says, in effect, "Here's your pension account; come and get it."

What the employer will offer you is called a *lump sum distribution*. It should include the employer's contributions and the earnings, plus your own contributions and earnings. Any after-tax contributions you made to the employer's tax-qualified retirement plan cannot be transferred or rolled over to your IRA. These funds must be withdrawn on a tax-free basis. However, the accumulated earnings from these contributions may be transferred to another tax-deferred retirement plan.

What used to be a simple matter of transferring lump sum distributions to an individual retirement account has now become a nightmare. One reason is that the U.S. Department of Labor found that only 13 percent of workers given preretirement distributions from their employers actually put all the money into other retirement plans or their own IRAs. In an effort to keep workers from spending the money they receive from their former employer's retirement plan, Congress adopted new rules for lump sum distributions.

When the amount you are to receive from the company's retirement plan is established, based on the vesting schedules and years in the plan, here are the options you have:

Keep the Money in Your Former Employer's Plan

Once you leave the job, the employer may not want to be bothered keeping track of your retirement account and may request that you take a lump sum distribution from the plan. That way, the company can clear your retirement account off its books and let you manage the money. However, many people feel the former employer can manage the money better. Another reason to keep the assets with a former employer is that tax-qualified plans such as 401(k)s are generally exempt from being attached in bankruptcies. This may not be true of IRA non-qualified assets.

Take the Money and Run

Under this option, the employer will withhold 20 percent of the money for part payment of future income taxes. If you are under the age of 59 ½, you will also have to pay an additional 10 percent early withdrawal penalty when you file your taxes (unless you are disabled or, in some cases, if you have a financial hardship). For most workers, this can be at least a 35 percent haircut just to take the cash.

Take the Money and Put It into an IRA

In this case, you will need to come up with the missing 20 percent that has been withheld so that you can make the full rollover to your IRA. If you don't come up with the missing money, the difference between what you receive in the lump sum distribution and what you invest in your IRA will be considered an early withdrawal and will be subject to regular income taxes. If you make up the shortfall and roll over the full lump sum into an IRA, you can file a request on your tax form for a return of the withheld money.

Roll Over the Entire Lump Sum Directly into an IRA

To do this, you have to give your former employer the name and address of your IRA trustee. If you don't already have an individual retirement account, you can open one without a contribution subject to the investment of the rollover. Then the employer can send the money directly from the company retirement plan to your IRA without withholding the 20 percent for taxes.

Take the Money and Use Income Averaging

If you were born before 1936 (at least age 50 on January 1, 1986), you may be able to elect special averaging of the ordinary income portion of the distribution. You must also have been a participant in the plan for at least five years. You can use this option only once in your lifetime.

Here's how it works: Assume that your income was received from five different persons (ten for 10-year averaging) in the current year, and that each of these people had no other taxable income. As a result, the lump sum distribution will be taxed at a low rate and not included as part of your other income for that year. By using income forward averaging, you can pay your taxes at these low rates rather than rolling over the money into an IRA and paying regular income taxes later on. Note that income forward averaging does not apply to TSA, 403(b) plans. If you want to use this option, see your accountant before you take the employer's lump sum distribution.

Keep the Lump Sum Money in a Separate IRA

If the rollover funds are not commingled with your other IRA investments and are kept in a separate IRA, you may be able to transfer this money to your new employer's retirement plan, assuming the new employer allows this.

Types of Company-Sponsored Retirement Plans

Here are the five principal tax-qualified retirement plans in order of the cost to the employer. Some employers may offer more than one plan.

Defined Benefit Pension Plans

Although many company retirement plans are referred to as "pensions," most workers today aren't covered by a pension. The word "defined" comes from the fact that the benefit at retirement is defined in advance. It is usually based on the average of the last five years' salary, the number of years of service and the age at retirement. Most defined benefit pension plans require the employer to take all the investment risks and make the necessary contributions each year so that when the worker reaches retirement age there will be enough money in the plan to pay lifetime monthly benefits.

Maximum annual deductible contributions: As much as is needed to provide the promised benefits at retirement, subject to dollar limits that are adjusted for inflation each year.

Defined Contribution Plans

The only employer obligation under this plan is to make a defined contribution for each covered worker. Since these contributions must be made each year, regardless of profits, the number of these plans is rapidly decreasing. These plans differ from defined benefit plans in that the employer offers no guaranteed benefits at retirement. The plans are often called *money purchase plans* because the retirement benefits amount to whatever the assets in the account will purchase at the time of the employee's retirement.

Maximum annual deductible contributions: 25 percent of salary or $30,000, whichever is less.

Profit-Sharing Plans

These plans make it even easier for a company to offer a retirement plan. Since the obligation the company has is to contribute part of its profits each year, if any, into each worker's account, these retirement plans are often more illusion than reality. What's more, the company can change the rate of contributions, based on profits, or eliminate them in any year. Monthly benefits are whatever the money in the worker's account will buy at retirement.

Maximum annual deductible contributions: 15 percent of salary or $22,500, whichever is less.

Employee Stock Ownership Plans (ESOPs)

Under ESOPs, the company typically makes its contribution with company stock, and employees can use their own contributions to purchase the company's stock by payroll deductions. ESOPs are a form of profit sharing, and the purchases of stock are made with before-tax dollars. You are not taxed on any gain until you sell the stock. Most ESOPs don't provide borrowing privileges or allow the withdrawal of cash until you leave the company or sell the stock.

Because the idea is to encourage employees to purchase company stock, ESOPs tend to vest more rapidly than other retirement plans. Consider participating in an ESOP only if you believe that the company has good long-term prospects. The risk in an ESOP is that if the price of the company's stock declines significantly, you could take a big loss on a major portion of your retirement nest egg.

Maximum annual contributions: 15 percent of salary or $22,500, whichever is less.

401(k) Plans

Named after the section of the Internal Revenue Code that sanctioned them in 1978, these retirement plans have become the darlings of the 1990s. They are popular with employers because they shift much of the financial burden of paying retirement benefits from the employer to the worker. In the process, the employer is let off the hook for the massive costs of pension guarantees *and* the investment risks inside the retirement plan. Unlike pension plans that guarantee a fixed benefit at retirement, 401(k) plans guarantee nothing. The benefit depends entirely on how much money has been invested and what it has earned when you decide to retire.

Employer contributions. A letter outlining one company's 401(k) plan put it this way: "The company is making it clear that employees must take responsibility for a share of their own retirement." To encourage employee participation in the retirement plan, many employers require the worker to first make voluntary contributions from his or her paycheck before the employers will kick in any money. In many cases, the employer matches the worker's contributions, say 50 cents or $1 for every dollar of employee contributions, up to, say, 6 percent of pay. In one 401(k) plan, for example, the employer matches the employee's contribution dollar for dollar on the first 3 percent of pay set aside and 50 cents on the dollar on the next 2 percent of pay. Under this formula, employees have to set aside at least 5 percent of pay to trigger the maximum match. Most 401(k) plans allow employees to make additional contributions on their own if they wish. For most people who want to save money, these long-term matching contributions make this a no-brainer "yes" decision. The reason is simple:

Suppose you save $3,000 of salary and the employer matches your contributions 50 cents on the dollar.

One-Year Growth Comparison

	401(k)	*On Your Own*
Amount saved	$3,000	$3,000
Less taxes @ 30%	0	(900)
Amount to invest, with match	4,500	2,100
Earnings, 1st year @ 10%	450	210
Less taxes @ 30%	0	(63)
Balance year end	4,950	·2,247

This is not a figment of your imagination. In the first year you actually save $3,000 and end up with almost $5,000. I know the bib overall farmers would jump at the chance of turning $3,000 into $5,000 in one year.

If you can save $3,000 each year for five years, and if the employer continues the 50 cents on the dollar match, you'll feel a cheery afterglow when you hit retirement.

Five-Year Growth Comparison

	401(k)	On Your Own
Amount saved	$15,000	$15,000
Less taxes @ 30%	0	4,500
Amount to invest, with match	22,500	10,500
Total amount @10%	30,220	12,920

Under this example, in a 401(k) plan, you are saving $3,000 a year for five years, yet each year you are, on average, earning $6,000 a year towards your retirement nest egg. I know you are thinking it's too good to be true. Besides, taxes have to be paid on the 401(k) money before it can be used in retirement. But under this example, the 401(k) account will amount to $21,154 after taxes, almost double the amount accumulated outside the plan.

It's never too late to get rich. If you use salary reduction and save $250 a month, $3,000 a year, for 15 years, from age 50 to age 65, and if the employer continues to match your 401(k) contributions 50 cents on the dollar, you can still retire with a hefty financial nest egg. Using our previous example, but assuming a 15 percent annual total return in our common fund, you end up with about $246,000 at age 65. That's a profit of over $200,000! Now brace yourself for this: Over this 15-year period, each year you save $250 a month, $3,000 a year, you earn, on average, a whopping $13,400—not in get-rich-quick schemes, but in stock mutual funds with a solid performance record.

How are you going to pay for this hefty nest egg? For many workers, the cost is little or nothing. Salary reductions into a 401(k) plan reduce your taxable income, and this could put you in a lower tax bracket. For many workers, the lower tax bracket could save as much as the 401(k) plan contributions. This lets you pocket the retirement plan contributions without spending a dime!

Difference between a 401(k) and a pension.   The key difference between a 401(k) plan and a pension plan is that the former is a *self-directed* retirement plan. Unlike pension plans that are run by big pension management firms, self-directed retirement plans are managed by the employee. He or she, not the employer, decides where and how to invest the funds in the 401(k) account. Under Department of Labor rules, employers offering 401(k) plans and other defined contribution plans are not responsible for employees' poor investment decisions if they offer at least three diversified investment options and allow asset shifts at least every quarter.

A 401(k) plan should offer the following menu of choices:

- fixed savings account or money market fund
- bond mutual funds
- stock mutual funds
- employer's company stock

It's worth reiterating that retirement plan contributions belong at least 80 percent in stocks. Otherwise, you are just feeding at the trough while the people who receive your fixed savings are pigging out by investing it in the stock market. Millions of workers haven't learned this lesson. According to the U.S. Department of Labor, which oversees employer-sponsored retirement plans, three-fourths of all workers with self-directed plans have none of their money in stocks. Only about 5 percent have 50 percent or more of their money in equities. A big share of the 401(k) money is invested in *guaranteed investment contracts*, which are sold by insurance companies and offer a fixed rate of return like a savings account.

Borrowing from a 401(k) plan. Almost two-thirds of employers who offer 401(k) plans also allow employees to borrow their own money from the plan. You may borrow half your vested account balance, up to a maximum of $50,000. While there is no required minimum, most companies set minimum loans from $500 to $1,000. Since this is a loan, the money you take out of the retirement plan is not taxable income. That's because you are expected to repay the loan, usually through payroll deduction at least quarterly, over five years. If you use the money to buy a primary home, you might be able to take as long as 15 or 20 years to repay it. The money you use to repay your 401(k) loan and the interest costs is not tax-deductible.

Borrowing from your 401(k) plan is usually permitted for emergency medical expenses, "hardships" and college costs. For young people seeking to buy that first home, becoming their own bank and borrowing from their own 401(k) plan for the down payment can be very attractive. As our example above pointed out, you double your initial savings pot, nobody checks your credit history, and the interest rate is usually very good. It's the fastest way I know to save for a down payment on a home. On the other hand, if you already own a home, a home equity loan is a better deal because you can deduct the interest and the rates are about the same.

If you have a loan from your company retirement plan and you leave your job for any reason, the entire loan can become due and payable on your departure. You can either repay the loan and then roll over your entire lump sum distribution into an IRA, or you can walk away from the loan. If you fail to repay the loan, it will be considered an early withdrawal from the plan and will be subject to regular income taxes and, if you are under the age of 59½, to a further 10 percent penalty.

Contribution limits. Maximum annual deductible contribution: 15 percent of salary or about $9,200 in 1994 (adjusted for inflation each year) whichever is less. Total company and employee contributions to each account may not exceed 15 percent of salary or $22,500, whichever is less.

TSA, 403(b) Plans

A rising tide lifts all boats, according to the common wisdom, but some boats float and some are left in dry dock. In this case, the tide left the individual retirement opportunities of most working Americans on dry land.

In the 1950s, teachers and workers at private nonprofit organizations such as hospitals and charitable foundations were not covered by a company-sponsored retirement plan or Social Security. As a result, Congress passed the Technical Amendments Law of 1958. Because the law covered only employees of privately supported nonprofit organizations, while excluding their counterparts in educational institutions supported by public tax money, the national teachers union launched a massive lobbying campaign to allow their members to step inside the tax-free elevator before the door was slammed for good. As a result, Congress amended the original pork barrel section of the act and created 403(b) accounts in 1961. Public Law 870 permits employees of public and private schools to take advantage of this gold-plated retirement program.

Tax-sheltered annuities (TSAs) work much like IRAs except that they are sponsored by the employer.

Investments.   Under current law, TSA participants can invest in an income plan with a fixed or variable insurance company annuity, known as a 403(b)1 account, or in mutual funds, known as a 403(b)7 account. Deposits into TSAs are not subject to federal or state withholding taxes, and there is no annual tax on accumulated earnings in the account.

Rollovers.   TSAs are portable benefit plans. A TSA account created at one employer can be taken with you when you change jobs as long as the new employer is a qualified nonprofit or educational institution. Funds can also be transferred directly from a TSA to another TSA without a tax consequence. At termination of employment, TSAs can also be rolled over into an IRA. IRA funds cannot be rolled over into a TSA unless they originally came from a TSA.

Withdrawals. Withdrawals from a TSA are made in the same way as from an IRA, but, unlike an IRA, you can borrow from a TSA for any reason. Current law allows loans of 100 percent of the first $10,000 of the account value, no loans between $10,000 and $20,000 and 50 percent of account values above $20,000 not to exceed $50,000. Non-real estate loans must be paid back within five years; with real estate loans, you can usually take up to 30 years for full repayment.

Contributions. If you or your spouse are covered by an employer-sponsored retirement plan and your earnings are over the limit, you can't make a deductible contribution to an IRA, but you can to a TSA. If one spouse is covered by a retirement plan at work and the other spouse is eligible for a TSA, tax-deductible contributions can be made into the TSA regardless of income.

You can contribute 20 percent of your salary to a TSA, not to exceed $9,500, but if you have more than 15 years of service with your current employer, the maximum cap is $12,500. With a $2,000 annual cap on IRAs, these limits are spicy prospects indeed. Even greater contributions can be made to TSAs under the "catch-up clause," which allows you to make up for years when little or no contributions were made. Contributions to TSA plans are made by a salary reduction agreement, whereby the employer actually makes the investments.

Types of Individual and Self-Employment Retirement Plans

The idea behind individual retirement plans was that if American workers saved on their own, they would be less dependent on Social Security and other government plans in retirement. To make saving money attractive to workers, the government offered the best incentive it has: immediate tax deductions.

Individual Retirement Accounts

The most popular game ever invented is Monopoly, but its appeal was not at first apparent. Retailers doubted that people would buy a game to make themselves rich, yet generations of Americans have sought to own Broadway and Park Place and to stay out of jail. When individual retirement accounts first appeared in 1974, for people not covered by a retirement plan at work, not many people were interested. To encourage more people to open IRAs, Congress made the deal even sweeter with the passage of the Economic Recovery Tax Act of 1981, which allowed *all* working Americans to make tax-deductible contributions to IRAs.

Then, in an attempt to raise more tax revenue to reduce the staggering federal budget deficit, Congress tinkered with the rules. Under the 1986 Tax Reform Act, many working people are once again denied a tax-deductible way to save on their own.

How many?   You can have as many IRAs as you like, as long as you don't take a tax deduction for more than the allowable amount each year.

Transfer.   You can transfer assets between different IRAs as often as you like. This is a "trustee-to-trustee" transfer, where you don't take possession of the money yourself. For example, if you want to change your IRA account into a new mutual fund, you can give the new IRA trustee approval to move the assets directly from the old IRA to the new one.

Rollover.   You can roll over the assets in your IRA to another IRA only once every year. You simply ask the IRA trustee for a cash payment or have the investments sent to you. Once you have the assets in hand, you have 60 days to select and invest in another IRA to avoid the taxes and withdrawal penalties. This rule applies to each IRA you have. If you have several IRAs, you can make several rollovers a year.

Regular or self-directed. A regular IRA is one in which you invest in products provided by the IRA trustee. For example, if you open an IRA at a bank and invest in its insured savings accounts, you usually pay no annual fee. Another example of a regular IRA is when you invest in a mutual fund and the fund company becomes the trustee. Some mutual funds, however, do charge an annual fee.

With a self-directed IRA you can invest in stocks, mutual funds or other approved investments. You can open the account with a brokerage firm, a financial planner, a bank or savings and loan. There is an initial setup fee and an annual maintenance fee, which can run $50 or more.

Where to invest. You can invest only in so-called "approved" investments in your IRA. One nugget buried in the 1981 tax bill does not allow you to invest in gold, diamonds, stamps, antiques and other collectibles. The House Ways and Means Committee, bowing to the bank and savings and loan industries, found that "collectibles divert retirement savings from banks and thrifts and other traditional investment media, and investments in collectibles do not contribute to productive capital formation." You can't invest in life insurance, but you can invest in U.S. Treasury-issued gold and silver coins.

If you have a stock that's doing very well and you'd like to put it in your IRA, you can't. The IRS doesn't allow contributions of existing investments to an IRA. Your only choice is to put in fresh cash and buy the stock on the open market.

Withdrawals. Here's a quick reference on the tax penalties for withdrawals from IRAs:

	Penalty
If you withdraw too little, over age 70 ½	50%
If you withdraw too much, more than $150,000 a year	15%
If you withdraw too early, under age 59 ½	10%
If you die with too much in the IRA, about $1 million	15%

Similar rules also apply to 401(k)s, Keoghs and other retirement plans.

Under the age of 59 ½. Generally, if you receive an IRA distribution before the age of 59 ½, you are required to pay a 10 percent tax penalty on the money withdrawn. There are several exceptions:

- death (paid to a beneficiary)
- total and permanent disability
- disbursements received in periodic payments over life expectancy or the joint life expectancy of you and your beneficiary
- separation from service during or after the calendar year in which you reached age 55
- court-directed divorce proceedings
- medical expenses, under certain conditions

Over the age of 70 ½. You can make contributions to an IRA until the age of 70 ½, and you can continue making contributions to a spousal IRA until your spouse reaches age 70 ½. When you reach the age of 70 ½, you must make withdrawals from the IRA or pay an excess tax of 50 percent of the minimum amount that is not withdrawn. You have two options: You can withdraw the entire amount, but if the total withdrawn in a year exceeds $150,000, a 15 percent excess distribution penalty can be levied. An alternative is to withdraw periodic distributions of the balance. In this case, you must start receiving distributions from your IRA by April 1 of the year following the year in which you reach age 70 ½. The minimum withdrawal is figured on your life expectancy or the joint life expectancy of you and your spouse. Currently, for a person age 70 ½, the IRS tables show a life expectancy of 16 years. Therefore, the minimum annual withdrawal is $\frac{1}{16}$ each year or 6.24 percent of the account value.

Contributions. If you have earned income—income earned on the job rather than from investments—you can contribute up to $2,000 a year to your IRA, or 100 percent of your income if it is less than $2,000. If your spouse does not work outside the home and his or her income is less than $250, and if you file jointly, the annual contribution limit is $2,250. No more than $2,000 of that amount may go into either spouse's IRA. If both spouses have earned income, they can each open an IRA and contribute up to $2,000 each. There is no minimum requirement for contributions to an IRA, just a maximum annual limit.

Not covered by a retirement plan. If neither working spouse is an active participant in a retirement plan at work, you can make the full $2,000 annual tax-deductible contribution regardless of your income. The Internal Revenue Service defines an "active participant" as someone who is "covered under or a member of any employer-sponsored retirement plan at any time during the tax year." In some cases, as with a defined benefit plan, you may be considered an active participant if the plan's rules say you are covered, even if you decline to participate.

Covered by a retirement plan. If you or your spouse are covered by a retirement plan at work, your ability to make a tax-deductible IRA contribution and to what extent will depend on your taxable income.

If you are single, you can make the full $2,000 tax-deductible contribution if your adjusted gross income (AGI) for the year is less than $25,000. Earning between $25,000 and $35,000, you can make a partial contribution. With an AGI over $35,000, no tax-deductible contribution is allowed.

If you are married, filing jointly, you can make a full tax-deductible contribution if your AGI is less than $40,000, and partial contributions between $40,000 and $50,000. Over $50,000, no deductible contributions are allowed.

If you fall within the $10,000 "window" in which only partial contributions are allowed—an AGI of between $25,000 and $35,000 if you're single or between $40,000 and $50,000 if married—here's how to calculate the amount you will be allowed to contribute to your IRA and take a tax deduction.

Let's say you are married and have an AGI of $42,000. Subtract that amount from the maximum of $50,000 and take the remainder—$8,000—as a percentage of the $10,000 window in which partial contributions are allowed. In this case, that means your allowable tax-deductible contribution to your IRA will be 80 percent of the maximum allowable contribution of $2,000, or $1,600.

If you are not eligible for a tax-deductible contribution, the law allows you to make up to $2,000 a year of nondeductible contributions into an IRA.

Basic Rule #22:

Make your IRA contributions early in the year.

Making contributions early each year and allowing the earnings to compound can boost your retirement nest egg by thousands of dollars at retirement. If you can't come up with the money all at once, use payroll deductions or other forced savings plans to get the money in as early as you can. Another tip that can substantially boost your final nest egg is to pay the annual IRA management fees yourself, not from the funds inside the account.

Check with an accountant, bank, broker or financial planner before you make a move. The tax rules for individual retirement accounts are now so complicated they fill 75 pages in the IRS tax manual. One letter I received from a reader of my newsletter sums up the mess Congress has created when he wrote, "It pays to know the ins and outs of IRAs because if you're not part of the steamroller, you're part of the asphalt."

Self-Employed Retirement Plans

Simplified employee pension.   You're at a cocktail party and one of your friends says he just made a tax-deductible contribution of over $4,000 to his IRA. How did he pull this off? You know he makes a fairly high salary and that he's covered by a retirement plan at work, so he can't make a tax-deductible contribution to his IRA. What he used, as a self-employed individual, was the "moonlighter's delight," a simplified employee pension plan (SEP-IRA). These plans work like IRAs and are, in effect, a cross between an IRA and a Keogh plan. If you maxed out on your 401(k) plan this year but have some part-time self-employment income, you can still drop a few thousand into a SEP-IRA and cut your taxes.

If you have self-employment income or own a small business, you can set up a SEP at the same places you open an IRA—with a bank, broker, insurance company or financial planner—and you can change the rate of contribution at any time. You can also establish a SEP-IRA on the cheap through no-load mutual fund companies such as Fidelity, Vanguard and T. Rowe Price, just as you would an IRA. If your business has other eligible employees, however, you must include them with their own separate IRA accounts and make the same percentage of pay contributions as you receive.

Investments. You can invest as you would with an IRA.

Withdrawals. Since the SEP-IRAs are really a form of IRAs, the same withdrawal restrictions and requirements that govern IRAs also apply to SEP-IRAs. If you change jobs, the good news is that you don't have to roll over the employer-sponsored retirement plan to your IRA, because you already have the funds in an IRA.

Contributions. The maximum annual deductible contribution for owners is 13.0435 percent of gross self-employment income; for employees it's 15 percent of salary or $22,500, whichever is less.

Only the Wonders in Washington can tell us why the annual tax-deductible contribution to a SEP-IRA can be more than ten times greater than to a regular IRA.

Keogh plans. These self-employment retirement plans are known as HR-10s, after the act that established them, but the more popular term is Keogh plan, after New York Congressman Eugene J. Keogh who was most responsible for the act's passage. Keogh plans were established so that small business owners could have the same type of retirement plans as large corporations. Unlike an IRA, a Keogh plan must be established before the end of your tax year in order to take a deduction for that year.

There are three basic types of Keogh plans:

Profit-sharing plans. As with any profit-sharing plan, the company can change or eliminate the contributions at any time. As with a SEP-IRA, you must include most other employees in the plan.

Annual maximum contributions: Same as a SEP-IRA.

Defined contribution plans. These are often called *money purchase plans*. This type of plan defines the rate of contribution (usually a percentage of income) that will be made to the plan each year. You can make larger contributions under this plan, but if you miss a year, the IRS can require you to make up contributions and can assess a penalty.

Annual deductible contributions: 25 percent of pay or $30,000, whichever is less.

Defined benefit plans. Like a pension, this plan pays a preset benefit at retirement. Defined benefit Keogh plans are very expensive to set up and operate, but it's possible for older individuals to put 20, 30 or even 50 percent or more of their income into the plan each year. This plan favors older workers, and the drawback for owners is that they must include other eligible employees in the plan.

Annual deductible contributions: as much as you need to build up a pension fund that will pay the benefit, subject to dollar limits that are adjusted for inflation each year. How much you can contribute each year will depend on your age at the start of the plan, your income and the actuarial assumptions on how fast the money in the account will grow.

Investments. You can make the same types of investments in a Keogh plan as you can in an IRA.

Withdrawals. A Keogh is subject to the same regulations on withdrawals as an IRA, but you can roll over your Keogh plan into an IRA.

Basic Rule #23:

It's up to you, baby.

You are going to have to feather your own nest and expect increasingly less help from company-paid retirement plans and Social Security. If this sounds a little cold-blooded, you're right. It is. Which brings us back to Basic Rule #1: Save 10 percent of your income first, and use part of those savings for contributions to your company's tax-qualified retirement plan. If you choose not to contribute to your company retirement plan, the chances are you won't save enough to live on in retirement.

CHAPTER 9

Finding a
Financial Planner

*Y*our financial plans are a mess. Your nest egg is not on bedrock, but crumbling as you travel toward retirement. At this point, you may start thinking about turning to a financial planner or broker for help. After all, you tell yourself, these are the pros in the money business. Maybe they know how and where to invest your money. The Consumer Federation of America, however, reports that the financial planning field is a minefield for consumers. At the heart of the problem is the fact that anyone can claim to be a financial planner and hang out a sign.

Originally, financial planning and money management services were aimed primarily at the wealthy, and the industry was based on "single-product" salespeople. Life insurance agents sold only life insurance, brokers bought and sold stock and bonds, and banks offered only savings accounts. By the 1980s, with financial deregulation loose in the land, financial advisers began invading each other's turf. Banks starting selling mutual funds, and brokers sold life insurance. As a result, insurance agents, brokers and banks now want to act as complete financial planners. But because these advisers didn't start out as multifaceted planners, they often push investors toward the product they know best, which may or may not be in the client's best interest.

Another group of so-called "financial advisers" works with employees in the area of company or association group benefits. They use monthly payroll deductions as a way to fund the insurance or retirement savings products. A classic case in point occurred in 1993, when a major life insurance company and its agents were charged by state insurance regulators with unethical practices in selling tens of thousands of whole life policies as a way to save for retirement. Many members of this group believed they had purchased an investment contract when what they actually bought was life insurance. A life insurance policy differs from other investment products, such as an annuity, in many ways.

The truth is, in the business of mass marketing, many salespeople are load-driven. The first-year commission for a whole life policy can run as much as 60 percent or more of the initial premium, an annuity from 5 to 6 percent. Because of these hefty commissions, the surrender cash value for the policy can be zero after the first year and only 35 percent after the second year. An annuity might have a surrender charge of around 5 or 6 percent of the assets withdrawn within the first year. These agents justify the retirement savings policies on the basis that they have a "plan completion benefit" in which the life insurance policy will complete the savings plan in the event of the death of the insured.

Basic Rule #24:

Do your homework before you use a financial planner.

The worst mistake you can make, and it could cost you a fortune, is to turn over your money to a financial planner without first understanding how the money is to be invested and what it will cost you to use his or her services. Also, before you trust someone to handle your money, find out all you can about his or her personal and professional reputation for integrity and competence.

You wouldn't allow a stranger to drive your car. Why would you let one handle your money?

Getting a handle on a good financial planner today is a lot like trying to roller skate in a room filled with marbles. Not only must you navigate a maze of investment products and indecipherable industry jargon (and often overly optimistic projections of what you'll earn), but you must also be sure the investments you do make will let you sleep at night.

Before you approach a financial planner, there are certain facts you need to know. Some planners are little more than single-product salespeople with little or no government and industry supervision. Others are professionals who face industry, state and federal government regulators. Some have little formal education, while others have a bachelor's or master's degree with professional designations. Unfortunately, federal regulators such as the Securities and Exchange Commission keep track of only a handful of planners. Many other people who purport to be financial planners report their activities to almost no one. Ideally, your planner should have at least four or five years of experience.

How To Select a Planner

Before you select a financial planner, here are some areas you should investigate.

Payment for Services

When you take your television set or car to be repaired, you get an estimate before the work is undertaken, but the cost of a financial planner's services are often vague, and they will depend on how the planner is paid. Before you start your search, decide what you want the planner to do.

Commission-only. Under this arrangement you pay no fees for the planner's services. He or she is compensated by sales commissions from life insurance, annuities, mutual funds, partnerships or other investments you purchase. A conflict of interest can exist when the planner depends entirely on commission income. Often, the riskier the investment, the richer the commissions, and the greater the incentive for the planner to suggest that you include them in your portfolio of investments. There is nothing wrong in buying these products, but you should be aware that commission income can differ, depending on the type of product. Planners also often receive *trailer commissions,* which are paid every quarter or year on the total assets in your account. If you select a commission-only planner, it's a good idea to ask for a written statement of how much he or she will earn for each type of product, and it's best to get this information before any work is performed.

Fee-based.   Fee-based, or fee-plus-commission, planners often charge a flat fee for advice and for working up a financial plan. They also typically earn a commission on any products they sell implementing the plan. The commissions often include annual fees for managing the assets. Once you have paid the planner's fee, you have no obligation to buy any products, but many planners will reduce their fees if you do.

Fee-only.   These planners work much like an accountant or lawyer, charging only for their time, at a typical rate of between $90 to $250 an hour. The initial fee to produce a financial plan can run anywhere from $500 to $5,000 or more, depending on the planner, your assets and your age. Although fee-only planners won't sell you financial products, they are often helpful in finding no-load or low-load investments, and they are free to suggest any financial investment. Before you select a fee-only planner, be sure to set limits on his or her hourly fees for the work you want done. Many fee-only planners can also provide a program to monitor your investments, usually for a charge of around 0.5 to 2.0 percent a year of the assets under management.

Salary.   Many banks, savings and loans and other organizations offer financial planning services. In most instances, financial planners on their staff are paid by salary and earn neither fees nor commissions. The financial institution is compensated through the sale of financial products or services. You are, however, often limited to the investment products that are available from that financial institution. Also, these planners may receive bonuses based on the volume and type of product they sell.

Educational Level

The initials after a planner's name do not guarantee competence or ethics, but they do indicate that the person has been in business for at least three years and has made the effort to learn his or her trade by completing a two-year, college-level course at a cost of about $3,000 for each designation.

The most popular professional designation is Certified Financial Planner (CFP). About 27,000 planners hold this designation, which is given by the International Board of Standards and Practices working with the College for Financial Planning in Denver. The college is an independent, nonprofit institution offering financial planning education and training. To become a CFP, a planner must pass a two-day, college-level exam and agree to follow a code of ethics. CFP holders must also complete 30 hours of continuing education every two years to retain the designation. CFPs, like holders of other financial planning professional designations, are not licensed or certified by any state agency.

The Chartered Financial Consultant (ChFC) designation is offered by the life insurance-based American College of Life Underwriters in Bryn Mawr, Pennsylvania. About 28,000 planners hold this designation. To maintain high standards, the College requires 60 hours of continuing education credits every two years. It also offers the Chartered Life Underwriter (CLU) designation for professional life insurance agents. Many planners hold both the CFP and the ChFC designations, and many also hold the CLU designation.

A financial planner may also be a Registered Investment Adviser under the Investment Advisers Act of 1940, and registered with the Securities and Exchange Commission (SEC). The SEC reports that about 19,000 planners have registered as investment advisers. A Registered Investment Adviser is required to keep detailed records and books and to follow specific guidelines for advertising and claims made to clients or prospective clients. Written communications sent by the adviser or received from the client must be kept on file for six years.

You can discount the fancy material you may receive from a planner. You want to focus on two documents: First, the disclosure statement, which must be given to a prospective client before any work begins. Among other things, the disclosure statement outlines the planner's services and fees, types of clients, education, background and other business activities. The second document is Part II of your planner's ADV form, which must be filed with the SEC and often the state. Sign each copy and retain one for your files.

Possible Conflict of Interest

Many planners work under contract to sell their firm's mutual funds and other products. You may not realize that many of the in-house products carry a higher commission than those offered by independent investment firms. In some cases, your investment could be a ticket to the next convention in Florida for the planner and his or her spouse. Most planners will tell you that they can recommend the best investment for you from any source, and many can, but it's a good idea to find out just how many financial products the planner regularly offers to clients. Hiring a planner who represents several financial firms does not guarantee that you'll make more money than you would with one who offers only one company's product. However, one of the things you are paying for is the planner's independent judgment, and that often involves surveying the entire field to find the best product for your individual situation.

Background

It's a good idea to find out whether the planner has ever been the subject of disciplinary action by any federal or state agency or professional body or been involved in arbitration proceedings with former clients. Any experienced planner will have worked with hundreds of clients and will have lost money for some of them. The investment business, with or without a planner's help, does not always produce big gains. Some clients don't fully understand the risks, or they expect their investments to skyrocket. When their investments turn sour, the planner is bound to get some complaints. Nevertheless, some planners have a list of complaints that goes well beyond the routine.

You can contact the National Association of Securities Dealers (NASD) to find out if a planner has been subjected to any disciplinary proceedings during the past three years by the SEC or NASD or to any criminal indictments by the U.S. Department of Justice. If the planner has had problems, the NASD will mail you the information. (NASD, Public Disclosure Program, Box 9401, Gaithersburg, MD 20898-9401, 800-289-9999.)

You can also call the North American Securities Administration Association (NASAA) (202-737-0900) for the number of your state's securities department. Your state regulator can enter the name of an individual or firm into a nationwide computer database maintained jointly by the NASAA and the NASD. The program, Central Registration Depository (CRD), tracks the person's education and employment history and indicates whether he or she has ever been the subject of a complaint or filed for bankruptcy.

Interview the Planner

After you have selected several financial planners for consideration, make an appointment to visit them in their offices. The initial visit normally is without charge. Here is where you learn what the planner can really do for you and whether or not you feel comfortable with the process. I suggest you pose a problem on how to invest some of your money. If the answer is in line with your comfort zone, you know you have a planner who thinks like you do. If the answer fills you with scary visions of financial ruin, you know you're in the wrong office.

It's a good idea to ask for the names of current clients with whom the planner has worked, but be careful that these names are not special clients who are sure to give a favorable report. Ask for a copy of financial plans that were tailored for clients with situations similar to your own. In the records, you can see whether the planner followed up and how skillfully he stayed on top of the client's lifestyle and financial changes.

Basic Rule #25:

Never take a recommendation you don't fully understand.

After you establish a relationship with a planner and receive his or her recommendations to invest in real estate, energy, commodities, partnerships or nonliquid long-term investments, take the time to consult a third party, such as a CPA or attorney, to determine the level of risk and whether the investment is appropriate for you. I often receive letters from readers who have plunked down tens of thousands of dollars in various high-yielding long-term investments that have gone sour. The cost of a few hundred dollars to run the proposal by an independent adviser first would have been the best investment they could have made to keep their nest egg intact.

Another pitfall to avoid is investing in something that is not suitable to your risk level or age. Here's one of many letters I've received from investors seeking safety and tempted by promised higher returns. The letter is from a 66-year-old lady who invested in long-term, high-risk and nonliquid limited partnerships in the 1980s.

> At that time, I told the broker I only wanted to invest in something very conservative since this was money I saved all my life working, and I did not want to lose it. This was money I needed for my retirement. He suggested the partnerships, and told me it was almost guaranteed so I could feel safe about it. The rest is history. Whenever I call him, he just says to hold on to them. I did, and now they are worth very little.

Remember, never make an investment decision in a hurry. If the planner or broker says it's a hot deal and they're almost out, pass. Often these planners are load pushers hoping the investor will listen to their pitch, rather than try to understand the possible pitfalls and risks.

Another trick used by a few commission-hungry brokers and planners is to encourage you to move from one mutual fund group to another. Before you do, find out whether the move is appropriate for you and if the sale of no-load funds you already own is to raise money to purchase funds with a front-end load.

In reality, most of us can't pull our own teeth or fix our television set, yet many of us can do our own financial planning. This is true in spite of the fact that the financial planning industry constantly tries to tell us that the job is too complicated.

Many people don't need a financial planner for the simple reason that they don't have enough money to make it worthwhile for the broker or planner to work on their behalf. Furthermore, most people can do the job themselves by simply investing in good-quality stock and bond funds. My bib overall farmer friends knew this. Since it was their hard-earned money, they took the time to learn about the products available and what risk they wanted to assume before they invested.

Nevertheless, many people feel they need the services of a financial planner. If you have over $50,000 (some firms now require only $25,000) to invest, one alternative is to hire a professional money manager for a fee to manage your portfolio of no-load mutual funds. These fee-only pros allocate your assets among stock and bond funds and fixed savings, depending on your risk level and income needs. They set long-term objectives, select asset classes, determine investment methodology and develop a strategic investment plan. One big advantage of working with these strategic asset money managers is that they keep you in the market at all times, avoiding individual stock selection and market timing. Their results of late, less their annual fees of 1 to 2 percent of the assets, have been top-notch. Most of these advisers provide reports and hold individual meetings each quarter with their clients.

Do-It-Yourself Mutual Funds

A popular excuse for many individuals who don't invest in the stock market is, "I just don't have enough cash to interest a broker. They won't even talk with me." To overcome this problem, I suggest you start your own mutual fund by buying common stock directly from the company. This lets you sidestep brokers' hefty fees and commissions for tiny transactions and small accounts.

For years, many companies have let stockholders buy additional shares directly from the company—like a no-load stock—by writing a check or by reinvesting the dividends. Dozens of companies now let investors buy their initial shares of stock directly from the company for a nominal fee or none at all. These companies include Exxon, W. R. Grace, Johnson Controls, Texaco, Dial and Arrow Financial.

Most companies, however, require an investor to be a stockholder in order to buy shares directly. To get started, you'll have to buy one or more shares from a full-service stock broker, a discount broker or the National Association of Investors Corporation (NAIC), the nonprofit organization that helps people start and run investment clubs.

Here's how the NAIC plan works: If a stock sells for $25 a share, NAIC requires an additional $10 to be added to that price, so $35 is earmarked for investment. The additional $10 allows for price fluctuations and assures that a minimum of one share is purchased. NAIC charges another $5 as a service fee for each company from whom you purchase stock. The plan has about 115 different companies from which to choose. To use the NAIC stock purchase plan, you must be a member of NAIC at a cost of $32 a year. Ask for the folders and applications for buying stocks. (NAIC, 1515 E. Eleven Mile Rd., Royal Oak, MI 48067, 313-543-0612.)

Another method of buying the first share is by joining First Share. A two-year membership with member handbook is $24. Once a member, First Share will help you buy a share from another member. You pay the market price, plus $7.50 to the seller and $4 to First Share. You can also agree to sell a single share of each company you buy to another member and receive the $7.50 service fee. For those who don't want to sell their shares, First Share's cost is $11.50, plus $7.50 to the selling member. Their directory of DRIP plans is $25.85. (First Share, 103 S. 2nd St., Westcliffe, CO 81252, 800-683-0743.)

After you are a stockholder in a company, you can build your own mutual fund by purchasing additional shares. The number of shares you buy each month is up to you; you can set the investment level anywhere from $50 to $500 or more. For 1994, you might consider building a stock portfolio that includes shares in General Electric, Procter & Gamble, May Department Stores, McDonald's Corporation, Caterpillar and Johnson & Johnson. These companies should continue to boost earnings and outpace much of the stock market over the next five years.

Once you own shares directly with the company you can also enroll in a dividend reinvestment plan (DRIP). This plan allows you to automatically reinvest the dividends in additional shares of stock, rather than taking the dividends in cash. DRIP purchases can often be made commission-free, and many plans give discounts of 1 to 10 percent off the current market price of the stock.

If you already own some shares with a broker, they are probably held in "street" name, or the name of the broker. You first must transfer them to your name and take delivery of the shares. The reason for the transfer of name is to eliminate brokerage commissions. Sometimes the DRIP plan will hold the shares for you, or you may have to take delivery and keep them in a safe place.

For more help, read Charles B. Carlson's book, *Buying Stocks Without a Broker,* published by McGraw Hill. Carlson also publishes a *Directory of Dividend Reinvestment Plans,* which includes companies that permit investors to make first-time purchases directly, all companies offering DRIPs and how to enroll in the programs. The directory is $13.95 plus $2 for shipping and handling. Order from Dow Theory Forecasts, Inc, 7412 Calumet Ave., Hammond, IN 46324-2696, 219-931-6480.

Evergreen Enterprises publishes the *Directory of Companies Offering Dividend Reinvestment Plans* at $28.95 plus $2.50 for shipping. Order from Evergreen Enterprises, Box 763, Laurel, MD 20725, 301-953-1861.

Do-it-yourself mutual funds are a great way for small investors to buy stocks in several different blue-chip companies and to build a portfolio over time on the cheap. Set aside some money each month and start your own plan now.

How To Find a Financial Planner

Referrals

Many people think they need a referral from a trusted adviser or friend in order to find a good financial planner. Word of mouth from someone you trust can be a good way to find a financial planner, but the person making the referral may know little or nothing about what the planner actually does. You might also get a name from someone whom the individual has known on a social rather than a professional level. And there is always the chance that the person making the referral is getting paid to pass along your name. For many people who don't work directly in the financial planning field, this is a good source of revenue. If this occurs, you are entitled by law to full disclosure before you approach the referral. Use referrals as a starting point and visit the planner, but do your homework before you agree to work with someone.

Commission and Fee-Based Planners

There are many excellent sources for finding a good financial planner. One of the best places to start is the International Association for Financial Planning (IAFP). Since 1985, IAFP has been a leader in establishing regulations for financial planners. Its members are expected to adhere to professional standards of ethics and practices. The organization maintains a list of the top planners in the nation, those who have met the highest standards in the industry for experience, education and practice knowledge. They are members of the *Registry of Financial Planning Practitioners*. For names and addresses of planners who have been admitted to the Registry in your area and various helpful booklets, contact IAFP, Two Concourse Pkwy., Suite 800, Atlanta, GA 30328, 800-945-IAFP.

The American Society of CLU and ChFC will send you a list of up to five professional planners in your area and a free consumer guide to financial services. (The American Society, 270 S. Bryn Mawr Ave., Bryn Mawr, PA 19010, 800-392-6900.)

Fee-Only Planners

The National Association of Personal Financial Advisors (NAPFA) is a nonprofit organization that advances the practice of fee-only financial planning. In order to belong to NAPFA, a financial planner may not receive any economic benefit when a client implements his or her recommendations, including (but not limited to) commissions, rebates, awards, finder's fees and bonuses. Members must also have either a CFP, ChFC or CPA professional designation and must complete 30 hours of continuing professional education each year. For a list of fee-only planners in your area and copies of their various booklets, contact NAPFA, 1130 Lake Cook Rd., Suite 105, Buffalo Grove, IL 60089, 800-366-2732.

The Licensed Independent Network of CPA Financial Planners (LINC) is a national organization of certified public accountants dedicated to independent, objective financial planning services on a fee-only basis. They offer a list of CPA planners in your area and a booklet on fee-only planning. (LINC, 404 James Robertson Pkwy., Suite 1200, Nashville, TN 37219, 615-782-4240.)

I don't know if you need a financial planner or not. After reading this book, you may decide you can start on your own and build your nest egg up to a point where it makes sense to engage a planner or financial adviser. The important point is that choosing a financial planner is similar to choosing any professional in whom you place a great deal of faith. If you feel things aren't working out right, don't hesitate to switch planners. You have no contract that binds you to any planner.

CHAPTER 10

Managing
Your Money

*M*any people overlook the importance of managing their money. At first glance, it may appear that we have no alternatives as to how we spend our money. After all, most of what we have to pay for today is so complicated it's enough to make the average person hyperventilate. But by taking a few steps you can calm down and review much of what you need to know to manage, invest, save and borrow more effectively.

Here are some ways to manage your money better:

Check Up on Your
Adjustable-Rate Mortgage

With interest rates changing frequently, many lenders make mistakes in the way they calculate monthly payments on adjustable-rate mortgages. "You would think banks would know how to add, subtract and multiply, but when it comes to making calculations on adjustable-rate mortgages (ARMs), they often make mistakes, and even a small mistake can cost the borrower a lot of money," says

Larry Powers of Consumer Loan Advocates (CLA), a non-profit organization that helps consumers with ARMs.

"Depending on what study you believe," he says, "there's a 20 to 80 percent chance you're paying the wrong amount each month. Of the 9,000 ARMs we checked, half were in error. Of those half, 22 percent were undercharging and 78 percent were overcharging the borrower, meaning that overcharging actually occurred in 37 percent of the mortgages audited." The average refund, Powers says, has been $1,588.

The problem with adjustable-rate mortgages started in the mid-1980s, when interest rates were high and "teaser" rates for the first few months of mortgage payments were the rule. The monthly mortgage payments are based on several factors, including rounding off, payment dates and the index used to calculate the interest costs. Another problem in calculating the correct payment for ARMs is the soaring resale of mortgages in the secondary market.

Errors can occur in a number of ways: using the incorrect index, calculating the wrong number of days between two interest change periods, always rounding up the rate by one-eighth of a point rather than to the nearest one-eighth or adjusting your payments on the wrong day of the month. If your loan was issued before 1986, new computer programs may incorrectly update your mortgage index or terms. Or, if your mortgage was sold to a different lender for servicing, the new computer programs may not pick up the terms of the loan correctly.

Although it costs a bit to find out whether your lender has made errors in its adjustable-rate mortgage calculations, once you've had it done, you can do it yourself in the future.

How To Check Your ARM

- Consumer Loan Advocates will do an initial audit of your interest rates for $119.95. You also get a 100-page manual with instructions for calculating your ARM in the future. The manual and video are $45, including shipping. (Consumer Loan Advocates, 655 Rockland Rd., Suite 106, Lake Bluff, IL 60044, 708-615-0024.)

- HSH Associates, a firm that tracks mortgage interest rates, offers a do-it-yourself ARM checkup kit for $3. (HSH Associates, 1200 Route 23, Butler, NJ 07405.)
- Loantech has been helping borrowers find errors in their ARMs since 1985. Its ARM CHECK service includes an audit of your mortgage and help in obtaining refunds from the lender for $95. A do-it-yourself manual is $17.95 plus $3.50 for shipping. (Loantech, Box 3635, Gaithersburg, MD 20885, 800-888-6781.)

Check Up on Your Bank

How safe is your bank or savings and loan? The sign on the front door of your bank or thrift assures you that "Each depositor is insured to $100,000." Most people think only of the safety of their deposits, which are insured by the Federal Deposit Insurance Corporation (FDIC), not the safety of the bank, but a failed bank or savings and loan could cost you a lot of money. A $250,000 savings account in one name with a bank that is rated "significantly undercapitalized" and later fails could leave you with $150,000 of uninsured deposits.

There are several ways you can protect your bank accounts, the simplest being to limit the dollar amount per account to $100,000 in any one bank. Be aware that several different banks may be owned by the same holding company, and all of these banks could count as one bank.

A second way to protect your money is to keep savings and checking accounts and certificates of deposit in different banks if their aggregate value is greater than the FDIC insurance limit. If you have $60,000 in a savings account, another $50,000 in insured CDs and $10,000 in your checking account, all in your name or a joint account at one bank, your total will exceed the $100,000 of deposit insurance. You can be hit with uninsured deposits if your spouse dies. If you had $75,000 and your spouse had $50,000 in separate accounts, upon the death of your spouse, your accounts would total over the $100,000 limit of insurance.

Consider how the FDIC limits will affect your IRAs, Keogh plans and other self-directed retirement plans. They are now FDIC-insured up to $100,000 in the aggregate in one named account, in any one financial institution, even though a single retirement account may hold a much larger sum. For example, if you have $50,000 in an IRA and $60,000 in a Keogh plan in your name at one bank, $10,000 is not federally insured. These new regulations apply to individual retirement plans but do not affect employer plans. Depositors will still be able to maintain the full FDIC coverage through different ownership arrangements. For example, a married couple could have their separate retirement accounts and a third joint account for a total of $300,000 of insurance protection.

Finally, to protect your money you must understand the risk of loss if your bank fails. If a banking institution fails, is taken over or is sold, you're likely to find that the previous bank's promises to pay you a certain interest rate on your deposit will no longer be honored. If you have a five-year insured CD paying 8 percent, the new bank may offer you only 4 percent. You have a choice: You can take out the money without an early withdrawal penalty, or you can accept the new lower interest rate. Also, you may suddenly find your line of credit or revolving loan reduced or canceled.

How To Check Your Bank's Safety

You can check up on the financial health of your bank or savings and loan through the following firms:

- Veribank charges $10 for a report on any one institution, $5 for each additional one during the same phone call, charged to your credit card. A written report for each bank is mailed to you after the phone call. Veribank uses a color code—green for excellent, yellow for fair and red for below standard. (Veribank, Box 461, Wakefield, MA 01880, 800-442-2657.)
- Bauer Financial Reports will tell you over the phone whether your bank is currently satisfactorily capitalized and meets all regulatory requirements. If your bank is a sponsor of their program you'll receive the bank's star rating and a summary report

for free. If the financial institution is not a member, the six-page report costs $35. (Bauer, Box 145510, Coral Gables, FL 33114, 800-388-6686, Monday through Friday, 8:00 a.m. to 8:00 p.m., eastern time.)

Check Up on Your Credit Rating

You may feel confident that you have excellent credit, so you believe there's no need to check your credit file. Wrong. An incorrect credit report can hurt you if you're trying to close a mortgage, get a personal loan or land a job. Consumer research groups have turned up massive mistakes in credit bureau files. Therefore, it's a good idea, like an annual trip to the dentist, to check your credit bureau report each year. It may be too late if you wait to correct your report until you are denied a new job or a new mortgage.

Spot checks by Consumers' Union found a 40 percent error rate in credit reports. "More than two out of five people have some erroneous information on their consumer credit report," says an executive of a mortgage firm. Even more shocking were the findings of the U.S. Public Interest Research Group (PIRG), a consumer watchdog group based in Washington, DC. In a sampling of 140 Federal Trade Commission (FTC) consumer complaints, PIRG found 61 percent were denied credit, jobs or mortgage loans because of errors in their credit bureau reports.

I no longer question the credit bureau mess after three walks on a financial high wire. When I applied for a home loan, my report showed, in error, that I already had a hefty mortgage. I found this out when the lender called me. "What are you doing?" he asked. "You already have a home mortgage." Fortunately, the loan was removed from my credit report in time to buy the new home. On another occasion, I applied for a gasoline credit card and, to my surprise, I was turned down. I learned that the credit agency had sent the oil company a credit report for another individual with the same name living in another part of the state. A few years later, when I applied for credit, I learned that I had supposedly already declared bankruptcy. Shocked over this turn of events, I found this time that my report included information on another individual who had declared bankruptcy and who had a birth date 14 years different from mine.

If this can happen to me, it can happen to you! Or consider this conversation I had on the air with one of my listeners:

"I've been out of work for the past 14 months and I finally found a great job. I had a great interview, and then I got the cold shoulder, a turndown."

"That's too bad," I said. "Do you know what happened?"

"Yes," he told me. "The employer asked to look at my credit bureau report, and the idiots sent one that was full of errors with things I never heard of. With my lousy credit bureau report there was no way they could hire me. By the time I got the credit report corrected, it was too late to get the job."

Even a simple misplaced letter or digit can stamp you as a deadbeat or cost you a new job opportunity. Most errors occur when credit information is applied to the wrong file, when people get mixed up in the computer. Even a misplaced Social Security number can slip you into another person's file.

What's in Your Credit Report?

Your credit report is a credit history. Firms to which you have applied or been given credit make regular reports about your accounts to the credit bureaus. If you are late in making a payment, or if you overdraw your bank account, the information can show up in your files. Your legal record may also be included in your report, including marriage, divorce, liens, bankruptcy and other matters of public record. Certain personal information can't be included in your credit bureau report, including medical information (unless you give your consent), bankruptcy after ten years and negative information about debts after seven years.

How Private Is Your Credit Report?

People spill their financial guts every time they apply for a loan or credit card, open a bank account or buy insurance. So it's no wonder that your credit bureau knows how much money you make, how much you owe, what credit cards you use and a lot more about your private financial life. Once the financial institutions have this personal data, they frequently use it themselves and sell the information to companies who want to market their products. Evan Hendricks, editor of the *Privacy Times* newsletter, says, "When you fill out an application, chances are the information will be sold."

By law, anyone with a legitimate business purpose can get access to your credit report. That means lenders considering whether to grant you credit, landlords, insurance companies, employers and potential employers. The simple fact is that almost any firm—direct marketers, mail-order companies, 900 telephone scam operators—can tap into your credit file. The concern today, says Hendricks, is the emergence of so-called "super bureaus," which buy credit information and personal financial data in bulk and then resell the information.

Recent changes in federal law and an avalanche of lawsuits have made it easier for you to check up on your credit bureau report. If you are denied credit, you are entitled to a free copy of your credit report. The rejection letter you receive will tell you how to order your free copy. You must request it within 60 days. Otherwise, you can order a credit report for about $8. If you find errors, you have the right to have them corrected. Negative information in your credit report usually can be removed when you maintain a good credit record over a number of years.

If you disagree with an entry in the credit bureau's report, the bureau must investigate and respond to you within a reasonable time, usually 30 days. Since the information in credit bureau reports is usually supplied directly by financial firms, retailers and other merchants, the best way to have a negative listing removed is to work with the firm that placed the information in your report in the first place. If you can't get the dispute resolved, you can put your side of the story in writing in 100 words or less, and the credit bureau must include that information in your file.

How To Check Your Credit Report

The three main credit bureau reporting services are TRW Information Services, Equifax Credit Information Services and Trans

Union Credit Information. TRW will send one free report each year; the other bureaus charge $8 per copy. To find out how to obtain a copy of your report call:

* TRW 800-682-7654
* Equifax 800-685-1111
* Trans Union 800-851-2674

Once the credit bureau receives your request, it must mail you a copy within five working days.

Bankcard Holders of America offers a helpful booklet, *Understanding Credit Bureaus*, for $1. It also publishes *The Ultimate Credit Handbook,* with information to help you establish credit for the first time, find the best credit cards and tell whether you're carrying too much debt. The book is $10 plus $3 for shipping. (BHA, 560 Herndon Pkwy., Suite 120, Herndon, VA 22070, 703-481-1110.)

Check Up on Your Insurance Company

Recent headlines have shown us that the once-solid insurance industry, which has provided protection and good investment returns for 150 years, is no longer a guaranteed place to put our money. Many changes have occurred in the past decade, and insurance companies' investment strategies in real estate and mortgages, once considered prudent, are now considered risky.

When you buy a life insurance policy or invest in a tax-deferred annuity, you want a company that is prudent, well disciplined and financially strong. Unfortunately, several major insurers have been taken over by the state regulators over the past few years, and several today are in weak financial shape. "It's a whole new ball-game," an insurance agent told me. "You need to check the financial condition of the insurance company before you look at the return."

One problem of insurance company solvency is that many insurance companies no longer just sell life and disability policies and individual annuities. A big part of their business has moved into hybrid products such as guaranteed investment contracts (GICs), in which millions of workers seeking the safety of an insurance company's fixed-income contract, have put their employer-sponsored 401(k) plans. Some insurers also sell guaranteed municipal bonds (muni-GICs), where investors buy the highly rated bonds based on the insurance company's guarantee.

The collapse of several large insurance companies in 1991, including Executive Life and Mutual Benefit Life, resulted mainly from bad real estate loans. The payoff to policyholders has been delayed (at this writing by more than three years) due, in part, to lawsuits filed by the investors in GICs and muni-GICs who are furious at the prospect of ending up at the back of the line when regulators agree to pay out what's left of the carriers' assets to individual policyholders. A recent suggested settlement to policyholders from one of the failed insurance companies was for 70 cents on the dollar now or 100 cents on the dollar if they keep the policy in force with the company for another seven years. Well, almost. They'd get back the full amount on the first $100,000 of their investment, and as much as 71 cents on every additional dollar.

Here's an example of how an individual consumer can be affected when an insurance company fails and is taken over by state regulators: Say you purchased an annuity from an insurance company with an interest rate of 8.5 percent. The annuity allowed you to cash out each year on the date of the contract with no surrender charges. That sounded like a good deal, but the next year the insurance carrier was taken over by the state regulators. The new carrier has a surrender charge, starting at 7 percent from the date of the takeover. The new interest rate is only 5 percent, and it may go as low as 3 percent. You can wait another seven years for the return of all your money, or you can cash out now and receive only 85 percent of your current investment, less the 7 percent surrender charge.

Unlike a bank and savings and loan accounts, insurance contracts are not protected by federal insurance. Rather, in most states, the insurance industry has set up state-run *guaranty funds*. Unfortunately, these funds, which have to assess other member insurance companies in the state to obtain money, have, for the most part, held an almost empty cash drawer when a major insurer fails. The only thing that's guaranteed is agony for the people who retire or who need their savings and find that they are locked up inside the failed carrier.

A typical notice issued to new policyholders by the state of California's Department of Insurance states:

> The California Life Insurance Guaranty Association may not provide coverage for this policy. If coverage is provided, it may be subject to substantial limitations or exclusions, and require continued residency in California. You should not rely on coverage by the California Life Insurance Guaranty Association in selecting an insurance company or in selecting an insurance policy.

With little or no protection from state guaranty funds, it's important to learn the financial rating system when you shop for an insurance policy or annuity. A company that touts an A+ rating from Standard & Poor's may sound like a good deal until you realize that A+ is the fifth from their top triple-A rating.

Credit Rating Equivalences

Rank	*S&P*	*Moody's*	*Duff & Phelps*
1. Highest	AAA	Aaa	AAA
2. Excellent	AA+	Aa1	AA+
3. Good	AA	Aa2	AA
4. Satisfactory	AA−	Aa3	AA−
5. Questionable	A+	A1	A+

Conservative analysts suggest that an insurance carrier rated below the fifth rating could be experiencing financial difficulty. A lower rating does not necessarily imply the impending insolvency of a carrier, but it does indicate the presence of factors that have warranted a lower grade.

How To Check Your Insurance Company

The best way to check up on your insurance company's current credit rating is a telephone call to one of the following rating services. You can do that for just the cost of the phone call from 8:30 a.m. to 5:30 p.m. eastern time.

- Standard & Poor's will give ratings for up to five companies over the phone. Individual company analysis is $25. Call 212-208-1527.
- Moody's will give ratings for up to three companies over the phone. Call 212-553-0377.
- For a more detailed report, Insurance Rating Services will send you the ratings from A.M. Best, Standard & Poor's, Moody's, Duff & Phelps and Weiss Research. Reports for up to three insurance companies cost $15. (Insurance Rating Services, Box 852, Southport, CT 06490, 800-497-6561.)

Look For a Good Mutual Fund

Choosing a mutual fund, with almost 5,000 funds to pick from, can be intimidating and confusing. Many of them seem too good to pass up. Most funds advertise their past performance, and it's true that most good funds with excellent returns tend to repeat this performance in the future. No guarantees, of course, but as of now, looking at past performance is one of the best ways of selecting a fund. Here are some sources to help you get started:

- Morningstar tracks the performance of mutual funds and updates its listings frequently. A one-year subscription to its letter, *5-Star Investor*, mailed every two weeks, is $65. (Morningstar, 53 W. Jackson Blvd., Chicago, IL 60604, 800-876-5005.)
- Fund Education Alliance is the association of no-load funds. It publishes a 155-page directory, *The Investor's Guide to Low-Cost Mutual Funds*, for $5 and an educational kit, *Directing Your Own Mutual Fund Investments*, which includes a 40-page workbook and a 60-minute audiotape, for $15. The book, tape and directory are $17.50. (Fund Education Alliance, 1900 Erie St., Suite 210, Kansas City, MO 64116.)
- Investment Company Institute is a trade group of all mutual funds. You can order *The Mutual Fund Fact Book*, which

outlines the industry and how it works, for $15 or *The Directory of Funds*, which lists about 3,700 mutual funds, for $5. (Investment Company Institute, Box 66140, Washington, DC 20035-6140.)

- Investability is a mutual fund education organization that provides floppy disks each quarter with information on the performance of 4,866 mutual funds. The disk provides hypothetical dollar worth figures with bar graphs and side-by-side comparisons. Virtually every open-end mutual fund, load or no-load, is included in the database with ranking for the quarter and for one-, three-, five- and ten-year periods. The disks cost $29 each quarter, $99 for one year. (Investability, Box 43307, Louisville, KY 40253, 502-722-5700.)

- Financial magazines sometimes publish special mutual fund editions. One of the best is *Forbes*, which lists its honor roll and tracks fund performance in both up and down markets. *Business Week* has special mutual fund reports and an annual guide to help you locate funds and navigate around sales charges and redemption fees. You can purchase the $14.95 book in bookstores or by calling McGraw Hill at 800-2-MCGRAW. Other magazines with special mutual fund reports are *Money*, *U.S. News and World Report* and *Fortune*.

Find the Best Way To Provide for College Expenses

In today's competitive job market, a college degree is a necessity. According to a Census Bureau study, there is a growing wage gap between Americans who have gone to college and those who have not. In 1991, a high school graduate earned, on average, about $1,700 a month, a college graduate, $2,600. At that rate, the cost of a college degree can be recovered in about two years.

Most money books tell you to start saving early for the soaring costs of a college education. That's true, but how much you need to save depends on what type of school your child attends and whether or not he or she lives at home. The current cost for four years' tuition and room and board at a state university is between $30,000 and $40,000. Costs can run between $90,000 and $110,000 at a private university. If you project these four-year costs out just ten years, the cost of a four-year education at a public university is expected to be $70,000, and for a private university, $180,000.

The important thing to remember is that college costs are rising by about 7 percent a year, while inflation is at a level of only about 4 percent. In general, the longer you have to save for college costs, the more risks you need to take. That's because a net after-tax return of 7 percent will just keep up with rising college costs. You should consider investing in growth and aggressive growth stock mutual funds. As the tuition and other costs draw closer, say within two years of college, I suggest you move into investments with less risk, such as balanced funds and income funds from which you can write a check or make a withdrawal as the need arises.

Once your college-bound student is in the ninth grade, you need to look into financial aid programs. This gives you a year to make decisions that affect the 1040 tax return for the year before graduation. That's important because, when your child is about to attend college, it may be too late to get your financial affairs in order.

Phyllis J. Wordhouse, a college-level financial educator, provides these tips on avoiding the most common mistakes parents make:

- Don't assume that you earn too much money to qualify for grants and loans. People assume the worst and don't even request the forms, or, if they do, they don't fill them out. With the federal government beginning an unsubsidized loan program similar to Stafford loans, families in the $70,000-plus income bracket will qualify for financial aid.
- Get the forms from the college's financial aid office, not from some well-meaning high school counselor. The federal government requires that all colleges and universities supply each student with a free federal financial aid form. Many schools also ask for a financial aid form (FAF), a family financial statement (FFS) and their own financial aid form. If you don't fill out the forms, you have no chance of receiving financial aid.

- Read the instructions sent along with the required forms carefully and follow them to the letter. Students often miss out because they miss the deadline, don't get all the signatures needed on the forms, forget to fill in every blank or forget the check that is required with either the FAF or FFS form.
- Believe you can't afford the college costs. In reality, your child's family contribution numbers are going to be the same, whether college expenses are $4,000 or $27,000. The higher the education costs, the more need you can prove—and qualify for.
- Don't pay scholarship search firms to locate grants and loan money. Most aid comes from just three sources: the federal government, the state government and the college.
- Make personal contact. Some federal funds must be allocated according to certain requirements, but there are unallocated monies over which the financial aid officer has complete discretion. It's a good idea to visit the financial aid department of the college your child plans to attend. You want the financial aid officer to remember you when the federal discretionary and alumni monies are available.

Here are some factors that can affect whether or not you qualify for financial aid and grants:

- The number of students your family has in college at the same time, even if they attend only six credit hours for one semester. This divides the parents' portion of the family contribution "pie" into more pieces and creates a larger "need."
- Whether or not your student has a job. Never require your child to give up a job, but remember that the assets he or she builds up will hurt your financial aid eligibility. Have the child use the earnings for necessities such as car insurance, gasoline, clothing and pizza.
- The amount of money held in your child's name. Conventional advice is to invest in the child's name in order to save taxes, but with more assets in the child's name, families that would otherwise qualify for aid and grants lose out, even after the tax savings are taken into account. That's because money you have saved in your child's name will be assessed heavily in deter-

mining aid and grants. Students are expected to contribute 35 percent of their assets each year toward the family contribution, while parents are expected to contribute only 12 percent of their assets.

- Size of your mortgage. You'll want to maintain as much mortgage debt as possible. The federal form doesn't request the residential home value, but the college FAF and FFS forms do require this information. Higher debt means lower equity—and greater need.

Students can also borrow money to help themselves through college. Unsubsidized Stafford loans up to $2,625 a year are available to underclassmen, with higher amounts for upperclassmen. No payments on these loans are required until the student leaves college. For more information, contact the school's financial aid office.

For a computer analysis and individual help, contact Phyllis J. Wordhouse, 409 Plymouth Rd., Suite 230, Plymouth, MI 48170, 313-459-2402. She also has a set of audiotapes on qualifying for college financial aid.

Another helpful source is Octameron Press. *Financial Aid Officers: What They Do to You and for You,* by Donald Moore, and *The A's and B's of Academic Scholarships* are two books worth their price. Purchase them in a bookstore or contact Octameron Press, Box 2748, Alexandria, VA 22301, 703-836-5480.

These are just some of the areas that offer opportunities for you to manage your money more effectively. You'll want to look at your own circumstances, needs and goals to find other places where you can make your money work harder for you. Wise money management is an essential element in building your financial future.

CHAPTER   11

Putting the
Pieces Together

Your first objective after reading this book should be to stop
worrying about money. I know that's not easy. As our nation slowly
recovers from the insecurities of the recession, many people worry
about paying their bills, saving enough for retirement or hanging
onto their paycheck as job cutbacks ripple across the country. And
if that weren't enough, most of us will live longer than our parents,
pay much more in taxes and rely less on company retirement plans
and Social Security. That means you have to manage your money
more carefully than ever before. The good news is that if you adopt
an overall financial plan and stick to it, you will save enough to
provide a wonderful lifestyle in retirement. But you need to get
started today.

People often ask me for advice on where to invest their extra
money, but when I take a closer look at their financial situation, I find that they're not ready to make investments. Instead,
they have become financially bogged down because they continue
to make the most common mistakes of personal finance—paying
too much interest, failing to set up a tax-deductible retirement plan,

failing to buy enough life and disability insurance and passing up opportunities to save money.

A sound strategy for financial security must contain these basic elements:

- **Priority**. Put yourself first and pay yourself first. Pay off your consumer debt so you can begin to build up your savings and create a firm financial base.
- **Time**. Extend your time horizon and look at your financial planning as a ten-year job. Tortoise investing is the slow but steady path to building wealth. Jackrabbit investing is the fast path to financial loss.
- **Perseverance**. Start an investment plan and then stick to it. To continue your savings plan, you can use automatic payroll deductions, you can send yourself a bill and pay your savings account each month along with the other bills, or you can use dollar cost averaging to add a regular amount to your investments each month.

The biggest dangers you face in later life are that you won't have saved enough money during your working years or that you may run through your savings with ill-timed investments. Remember, if you spend before you save, you're not going to retire on someone else's savings.

Fidelity Investments' 1994 Retirement Pulse Poll found the percentage of participants that would be willing to reduce personal spending to save more for retirement dropped from 74 percent in 1993 to 54 percent in 1994. In addition, the mean amount by which the 1,400 survey participants said they would be willing to reduce personal spending dropped from $4,158 in 1993 to only $2,985 in 1994. "Apparently Americans have developed a false sense of security about their retirement savings," Fidelity said, "and think they don't have to curb their spending now to save more for the future." In fact, this survey suggests that Americans are not getting the job done and are facing an increasing danger of outliving their retirement savings.

Financial planning is like baking a cake. If you leave out some of the ingredients, the cake won't rise. If you leave out some basic elements in building your nest egg, your financial worth won't rise either. In fact, learning how to manage your personal finances is often as important as the money you have to invest.

Most people I talk with make financial planning and investing too complicated, and it's easy to see why. They are bombarded by brokers, newspaper advertisements and investment gurus who offer the latest sure-fire undiscovered stock, a way to double their earnings in some remote corner of the earth or the impossible dream of high returns with low risk.

Here are the steps you need to take, in order of priority, to build your financial future:

Step 1: Establish a Budget

In order to save money, you need to establish a workable budget and stick to it. The purpose of a budget is to force monthly spending levels below current income. For many people, the word "budget" means skimping, passing up the good times, depriving themselves. But that can be just the opposite of what happens when you stick to a budget. Most people don't find it fun to worry about paying bills or running out of money before the next paycheck. With a budget, you get more—not less—out of the money you earn. Here are some points to remember:

- Put your budget in writing. You must write down your budget and keep it in a visible place where you can continually check up on your progress. A budget put away in a drawer is a dead budget.
- Amend your budget as necessary. No matter how dedicated you are to staying within your budget, your life and personal finances will change and you'll have to make adjustments.
- Stay within your budget each month. Devise a budget that is workable for your current situation and then develop the discipline to stick with it. My recommendation is for a monthly budget that lets you save 10 percent of your monthly income for retirement plan contributions and personal investing, but you can work up to that level as you develop your saving habits.

Here's a guideline you can use for family finances: Most mortgage lenders have a maximum limit of 28 percent of gross income for mortgage payments, taxes and insurance, and no more than 36 percent of monthly pretax income for all personal debt.

A budget that lets you save first should also provide a cash reserve when an emergency strikes. Therefore, your first step should be to establish an emergency fund equal to at least six months' income. After that, in your younger years, the money you save might go into separate funds to pay off your personal debts or make the down payment on a car, or you might put the entire sum into a down payment on a home. If you are in mid-life, 5 percent or more might be used to pay off credit card and other personal debt first, and after that, into an investment plan.

For this safety net, don't keep six months' living expenses in a checking account. Instead, keep part of the money in a savings account and a higher-yielding short-term bond mutual fund. Part of your emergency money can also come from other sources. You can open a home equity credit line in advance of need, while you have a good job, and then keep it for emergency use. It's always a good idea to open a credit line when you don't need it because after a financial emergency, the bankers will probably slam the door in your face. A second option is to draw on your individual investment in mutual funds. If you have a profit in the securities, you'll be hit with taxes, but if you lost your job, your income could be less, and it might be a good time to realize the gain. As a last resort, make withdrawals from your tax-qualified retirement plans.

Step 2: Pay Off Your Personal Debt

Does your credit card pop out of your wallet as if it were hooked up to radar when you approach a shopping center? Does your monthly statement look as if you've been on a spending spree through Monte Carlo? Do you find it impossible to pay off your credit card balance each month? These are clear signals that you need to pay off your credit card and other personal debt. This is one of the key factors in starting a saving plan. Once you bite the bullet and pay off your personal debt, you'll be surprised how easy it is to find the money in your budget to invest.

As I've said before, the old-fashioned ways are often the best. Those farmers in their bib overalls paid cash. The reason? They knew the value of money. For example, let's say you have $100 in credit card debt and, at the same time, you have $100 invested in an insured certificate of deposit paying 4 percent a year in interest. The value of money works out like this:

The cost of $100 of credit card debt, at the national average card interest rate of 16 percent, is $16 a year. Since this interest expense is no longer tax-deductible, you need to earn, in a 30 percent federal and state income tax bracket, about $23 to pay the credit card interest expense.

The income from $100 in an insured CD earning 4 percent will return $4 at the end of the year. The after-tax return is about $2.80. If you withdrew the $100 from the savings account and paid off the credit card debt, you would be ahead about $20 at the end of the year. Or, to put it another way, if you are racing along the freeway of prosperity taking home $2.80 while paying out $23, you are headed for a big-time financial crash.

Step 3: Pay Yourself First

Once you've established a workable budget and eliminated your high-interest debt, you can begin to pay yourself first. Remember, your goal is 10 percent of your earnings. That doesn't mean you have to do that from day one. It will probably be easier for you to phase in your self-payments, perhaps beginning with 5 percent and then increasing the amounts until you reach your goal of 10 percent. Don't even think about the 10 percent that has already come off the top. You may have a smaller amount to manage, but you'll have a much greater motivation to manage it wisely and make it stretch to cover your basic needs and at least some of the extras we all desire from time to time. Remember, if you think you're going to save what's left over at the end of the month rather than paying yourself first, you just threw a bucket of cold water on your plans to build a realistic financial nest egg.

Step 4: Buy Adequate Insurance

Your next priority in building financial security is to protect yourself and your family from loss of income. To do this, you need to purchase adequate life insurance and long-term disability protection for your family. Even though life insurance protection is very inexpensive, most of the people I talk with at my investment seminars want to *invest* for the future rather than *protect* the future. They either rely on their temporary group life insurance at work, which can often be far less than their family will need in the event of their death, or they overlook this basic tool of protection.

The other basic element of family security is long-term disability insurance. A disability can rob you of a regular income and erode your savings in less than a year. Planning for the future is as important as planning for the unexpected. Without this protection, the best plans to build financial security can crumble and leave you and your family on food stamps.

Step 5: Safeguard the Money You've Already Saved

Unlike their parents, who were likely to stay with a company for 30 years and retire with a gold watch, this generation of workers will change jobs as many as six or seven times and will change careers as many as three times in their lives according to the U.S. Department of Labor. This represents a fundamental change in the workplace. The reasons for frequent job changes are many: The personnel office is doling out pink slips, there is a better opportunity with another company, or the worker is forced to take early retirement. The important point to remember is that, for most people, the days of a traditional company-paid pension are past. If you don't roll over your company retirement plan assets into an IRA each time you change your job, you won't have a pension at all.

These turbulent times aren't for the meek, and they are not for the average worker who squanders his or her future retirement assets changing jobs. Consider the findings of this recent study: Of the recipients of preretirement lump sum distributions from their 401(k) or other company plans, only 11 percent rolled over the entire amount into an individual retirement account. Around 55 percent rolled over part of the money, and 34 percent spent the entire lump sum as fast as they got their hands on the cash.

If you withdraw your lump sum distribution and you are under the age of 59½, you'll probably end up giving Uncle Sam at least 35 percent of the cash. For example, let's say you are changing jobs and the lump sum distribution from your company retirement plan is $10,000. Let's also assume that you invest in a stock mutual fund that has a annual total return of 15 percent and that you are in a 33 percent federal and state income tax bracket. Here's what could happen by investing the $10,000 on your own and inside an IRA when you reach age 65:

	Take the Cash *Pay Taxes*	*Roll Over to IRA* *Delay Taxes*
Start at age 35	$116,200	$662,000
Start at age 45	44,840	163,680
Start at age 55	17,230	40,460

As this example shows, nothing works faster than keeping the money you've already saved and making it work for you inside a tax-qualified retirement plan.

Step 6: Take Advantage of Your Employer's Retirement Plan

A big factor in building your retirement nest egg is your ability to participate in your company's tax-qualified retirement plan. If you don't take maximum advantage of these plans, it's like giving a big chunk of your money to Uncle Sam. If you are self-employed, consider Keogh plans and SEP-IRAs.

One big reason most people don't build a retirement nest egg today is that nearly half the employees eligible for 401(k) plans don't contribute anything. Without a self-paid pension, a lot of these free-spenders will bag groceries to get by after they retire. Regardless of what tax-deferred plan you select, start contributing now. It will require a small sacrifice each month by payroll deductions, but with the magic of compounding and forced saving you can end up with a sizable sum for your golden years.

Step 7: Be Willing To Accept Some Risk

One of the biggest problems most people face when they invest for their retirement is the fear of losing their hard-earned capital. "Risk" is a four-letter word that most investors would rather not hear about. As a result, billions of dollars are slumbering in low-yielding insured savings accounts and Treasury bills. After paying taxes on their income from these "safe" savings, the investor actually can lose purchasing power from year to year. For example, a "safe" 5 percent income can be wiped out by 1.5 percent in taxes and 4 percent inflation in a year. It's like running on a treadmill to oblivion. You are moving fast, yet falling behind.

Most people confuse risk with volatility. Risk is the possible loss of principal. Volatility is the possible change in the market value of a investment. For example, $1,000 invested in an insured CD is certain to return the original $1,000. Thanks to Uncle Sam, through the FDIC, there is no risk of loss of principal. There is also no volatility, since the investment is always worth $1,000.

Investing in the stock market, on the other hand, has a risk of principal, especially if you withdraw your money within a one- or two-year period. The market value of your investment can also change from time to time. When you put your money into a savings account, you pay for this lack of volatility and risk by giving up any opportunity for appreciation of your investment. This is a major factor in sharply reducing your ultimate retirement nest egg.

The important point to remember when you save for retirement is that you are investing long term. Consequently, you don't need to be concerned with the stock market's ups and downs. Your job, in what may appear to a savings account investor as a mission impossible, is to be courageous and realize that when an ugly bear market occurs, as it did three times in recent memory—in 1973–1974, the big crash in 1987 and again a mini-downturn during the Persian Gulf war in 1991—you can confidently ignore the bad news and stay invested in the stock market.

Stock market corrections are not new. They have been occurring since traders began buying and selling stocks in a coffeehouse near what later became known as Wall Street. What takes patience and courage is to put your head in the sand while everyone is losing theirs and wait for the market to bounce back and once more soar to new highs. In fact, when there is bad news on Wall Street and other investors are dumping their stocks, that may be the best time to buy. Another old Wall Street axiom is to "buy when no one wants to buy and sell when no one wants to sell."

Investing for the Long Term

Over the past 20 years, there was just one five-calendar-year period—between 1972 and 1977—when you would have lost money owning the stocks that make up the S&P 500 stock index.

Over a ten-year period there is almost no probability that a loss will occur in stock mutual funds. In fact, based on past performance, investing in a solid stock mutual fund for at least ten years is as close to a sure thing as you can get to reap a rich harvest in the years to come.

By comparison, during this ten-year period, while the S&P 500 stock index had an annualized return of 17.6 percent, safe 30-day Treasury bills had an annualized rate of return of 7.7 percent. Inflation, as determined by the consumer price index, averaged 3.9 percent a year. The net effect of playing it safe over this ten-year period was an annual return, after inflation, of only 3.8 percent for Treasury bills and 14.1 percent for stocks.

Many people ask me when is a good time to invest in the stock market. It looks like it's soaring or going down in price, and they want to catch it at just the right time. The good news is that when you invest long term you don't need the financial clout of a major Wall Street firm, you don't need to pick just the right time, but you do need to avoid becoming so stodgy that you avoid taking any risks at all. A calculation on stock prices showed that an investment of $5,000 in each of the past 20 years in the S&P 500 stock index made at the worst possible time each year—the day the market peaked—would have grown to around $500,000 from a total investment of $100,000. The fact that investing on the very worst day can produce so much profit tells us that we don't need to worry about short-term stock movements.

A similar calculation for bond funds found that investing $5,000 over 20 years at the peak of the bond market each year would produce around $300,000. Even with such relentlessly bad timing, shareholders would have tripled their investment. The reason is similar to the stock principle: Every year, although the investment fell the day after the new money went in, the combination of yield and price changes, plus the regular annual investment, soon took the total value beyond the previous peak. The risk for those who are willing to invest regularly over time is relatively small.

Step 8: Keep Your Hands Off Your Investments

After 30 years of watching investors rush from fund to fund, from hot stock to hot stock, from oil to gold to biotech, to the latest bond or stock fund invested in a country somewhere south of the equator, I have observed that most investors lose money while the financial advisers pay their rent and buy the BMWs. The problem is that most people feel they have to be doing something, accepting someone's advice, to make money with their investments. Keep another old Wall Street saying in mind when you think you should continually change your investments: "The investment that requires the least intervention will over time produce the best results."

The simple message is this: All the books that tell you what stocks to buy, the host of market timing newsletters that tell you when to buy and sell, or your broker's advice to buy a hot stock or to get out of the stock market, will almost always underperform a standpatter who stays fully invested.

A Beginner's Approach to Investing

John Bogle, chairman of the second largest mutual fund company, Vanguard Funds, talked to me on the air about his new book, *Bogle On Mutual Funds*. He believes that investing is not nearly as difficult as it looks. Bogle's advice: "If an investor will just buy a general money market fund with the lowest cost, a bond index fund and a stock index fund, he owns the three big asset allocation classes that he needs to own and really only needs to think about what portion of each his portfolio should be composed of. A new investor would do well to avoid the hassle of worrying about his or her investments and take the 'passive management' route."

History tells us that passive funds, such as index funds, almost always outperform managed funds that use portfolio managers who frantically search for the latest stock or bond investment and try to time the market. In fact, if your return was no better than the S&P 500 Index over the decade of the 1980s, you would have outperformed well over two-thirds of all managed stock mutual funds and beat most money managers who tried to outguess the market.

Index funds are a lot like IRAs, except you *do* pay taxes on cash dividends. Once invested, these funds don't buy and sell securities, so there is little capital gains tax to pay as profits are realized over the years. If they declare a dividend, that's taxable; but for the most part, index funds result in more of your capital at work for a longer period of time. Since index funds also don't have to pay for high-priced portfolio managers, stock trades and other expenses, they have sharply lower annual management fees. An actively managed stock fund might have an annual management fee of 1.5 percent *more* than an index fund's fees, so the fund managers have to outperform the market by at least this amount just to match the index fund's results.

Following up on Bogle's investment advice, depending on your age, you might want to put 10 percent of your money in a money market fund, 60 percent in an S&P 500 Index fund and 30 percent in a bond index fund. Vanguard, for example, offers four bond index funds that seek to replicate the total universe of investment-grade, fixed-income securities as measured by the Lehman Aggregate Bond Index, the widely recognized benchmark of the domestic bond market. You can choose from a low-risk, short-term bond portfolio with an average maturity of 2.9 years, a medium-risk, intermediate-term with a 7.5 year average maturity, a high-risk, long-term with an average maturity of 23 years and a total bond market portfolio with a medium risk and an average maturity of 9 years.

With interest rates set to rise in 1994, an intermediate-term bond index fund should double your insured CD yield with a low to medium risk. The fund plans to invest 62 percent of the money in U.S. Treasury and govenment bonds and 38 percent in investment-grade corporate bonds. Bond index funds also deliver higher-grade securities at lower cost. Vanguard's bond index funds, for example, are expected to maintain an expense ratio (expenses as an annual percentage of average net assets) of 0.18 percent—less than one-fifth of the 1.06 percent average expense ratio for actively managed, taxable bond funds as reported by Lipper Analytical Services.

Investing for Tax Reasons

Avoid selecting investments simply for tax reasons. Saving taxes is always a factor to be considered, but it's not smart to be driven by the tax code. It's a good idea to invest in tax-qualified retirement plans, both as a way to delay taxes on the original investment and the earnings and as a forced way to save. However, it's a bad idea to make investments simply to delay or avoid taxes.

Under our current tax code, there are only four ways you can delay or avoid taxes.

Tax-free income. Tax-free income is limited to that from municipal bonds. There are two kinds of municipal bond funds: single-state and nationwide. If you live in a state with a personal income tax, a single-state municipal bond fund made up of bonds issued in your state should allow you to earn interest income that is free of federal, state and local income tax. If you live in a state without a personal income tax, you can invest in nationwide tax-free bond funds and avoid federal income taxes.

Tax-deferred income. You can defer income taxes on your profits and capital gains when the investment is held inside a tax-qualified retirement plan or in a tax-deferred annuity or life insurance policy issued by a life insurance company. Because you are only deferring the taxes, the profits will be taxed at the current rate when the money is withdrawn. The right to defer taxes, however, can carry with it the risk of a 10 percent IRS tax penalty should you withdraw the money before you reach age 59½.

Tax-sheltered income. Tax-sheltered investments allow you to build up untaxed capital gains. The theory is that, since you have not sold the asset and consequently have not yet realized a gain, the value of the asset may decline in the future. For example, in a stock mutual fund, the increased value of your investment grows untaxed until you sell the shares. If the fund declares a cash dividend, however, this income is taxable in the year made. In real estate, the capital gains on the increased value of the property remains untaxed until the asset is sold.

Tax credit. A tax credit is as valuable as gold. Unlike a tax deduction from your current income, a tax credit reduces your tax liability dollar for dollar. For example, a $1 tax credit reduces your tax payments to the IRS by $1. A $1 tax deduction only reduces by $1 your adjusted gross income on which your taxes are based. Congress has authorized tax credits to encourage people to invest in certain activities such as research work, housing for low-income renters, work on alcohol used as fuel and wind machines for electric power.

If you follow the eight steps of financial planning, you can forget about worrying over your future retirement nest egg. Instead, you will have the money you need to play golf, take the kids to Disneyland, and enjoy life. There are no guarantees, of course, but after years of working with people and helping them plan their financial future, I am convinced that this is the best overall plan to build your financial security. It's not a plan to maximize your potential profits; that takes active effort and luck and many investors will do better. But if you are just getting started, or if you want a "hands off" savings and investment program, I suggest you consider this approach.

Where Will the Money Come From at Retirement?

When you retire at age 65, and you want to maintain your current standard of living (about 70 to 80 percent of your preretirement income), you can expect from 20 to 25 percent of the money to come from Social Security, about a third from retirement plans—yours and a company plan—and about 40 percent from savings. If you retire early, at age 62, with sharply reduced Social Security benefits, as much as 85 percent of the money you'll need will have to come from retirement plans and your own savings.

If you retire in 2008, 14 years from now, your normal retirement age for Social Security will be 66, and in 2027, 33 years from now, the retirement age will be 67. What's worse, these retirement ages are sure to increase in the future as Congress gradually ratchets up the normal retirement age, and early retirement benefits will take a hefty cut, somewhere around 70 percent of those available at the normal retirement age.

Again, consider the words of former Social Security commissioner Dorcas R. Hardy. "Baby boomers should think of Social Security benefits as a true 'floor of protection,' at best, and not plan for anywhere near the largess their parents received."

In closing, I want to share one of Aesop's most well-known fables.

As the story goes, the industrious ants worked night and day, storing food away for the coming winter. And all the while the foolish grasshopper strummed away and called the ants a bunch of silly fools. When winter arrived, the shivering grasshopper came begging for some bread, and the ants had to tell him, "We're sorry, but you should have taken the long-term view. There's no food to spare."

My own philosophy is that you don't have to live like the plodding ant in order to build your financial future, provide your children with an education and assure your own comfortable retirement. You can dance and make music like the grasshopper so long as you manage your money wisely and maintain a sound financial plan. You already have a powerful means of reaching your goal of building a secure financial future—your own subconscious mind. Most of us have had the experience of going to sleep at night with a difficult problem revolving in our minds and then waking up in the morning with a clear answer. That's the subconscious at work.

Take a few moments to relax. Close your eyes and think about what you want to accomplish. See your goals in your mind—a steady growing nest egg, freedom from debt, a workable worry-free budget, with your spending under control and money available for the things you need. Imagine that you are there, that you actually have these goals in your grasp. How would you feel? Let yourself enjoy those feelings of peace of mind, confidence in the future, satisfaction, accomplishment.

Now draw back to where you are now and look at the steps you will need to take to actually reach your goals. You know what they are. That's what this book is all about. Eight simple steps, each within your power to accomplish:

1. Establish a budget.
2. Pay off your personal debt.
3. Pay yourself first.
4. Buy adequate life and disability insurance.
5. Safeguard the money you've already saved.
6. Take full advantage of retirement plan opportunities.
7. Be willing to accept some risk.
8. Leave your investments alone and let time work for you.

Remember, like baking a cake, you can't pick and choose what steps you'll follow. To be successful in building your financial security, you need to start with step one and finish with step eight.

Take a few moments each day to repeat this exercise of visualizing your goals, imagining success and reviewing the steps to take. This will keep your subconscious on the job. You'll find yourself discovering more opportunities for saving, making better spending decisions and managing your finances better. You're no longer focused on worry, fear and anxiety. Instead, you're feeling more and more confident as you build your financial future day by day.

GLOSSARY

accrued interest.   Interest that has been earned but is not yet paid or payable.

accumulated dividend.   Dividend due the shareholder but not paid.

actuarial table.   A statistical device showing life expectancy.

adjustable-rate mortgage (ARM).   A type of mortgage in which the interest rate may change over time. *For contrast, see* fixed-rate mortgage.

adjustable-rate mutual fund (ARM).   A type of mutual fund that invests in adjustable-rate government-backed mortgages that let the rate adjust with market conditions so the share price remains fairly stable.

adjusted gross income.   Relating to income tax, gross income less certain allowable deductions.

after-tax return.   The interest, dividend and/or profit on an investment that is left after applicable taxes have been paid. *For contrast, see* before-tax return.

A.M. Best.   One of the rating services, specializing in insurance companies.

American depositary receipt (ADR).   A certificate representing an interest in the shares of a foreign-based corporation, issued by the bank or broker holding the underlying shares.

American Stock Exchange (AMEX).   One of the main securities exchange markets, based in New York City.

amortization.   The allocation of cost of an asset over its estimated useful life; the reduction of debt by regular payments of principal sufficient to pay off a loan by maturity.

annual effective yield.   The total interest earned over one year expressed as a percentage. This will be the stated rate if the account is based on simple interest. It will be greater than the stated rate if the interest is compounded during the year.

annual percentage rate (APR).   The cost of borrowing money, expressed as an annual percentage.

annuity.   A contract or agreement providing for periodic payments, either for life or for a term of years. *See also* deferred annuity, fixed annuity, immediate annuity, joint and survivor annuity, split annuity, tax-deferred annuity, variable annuity.

ARM.   *See* adjustable-rate mortgage, adjustable-rate mutual fund.

asset allocation fund.   A type of mutual fund that spreads its portfolio among a wide variety of investments, including domestic and foreign stocks and bonds, government securities, gold bullion and real estate stocks, thus offering broad diversification to small investors.

authorized issue.   The total numbers of shares of capital stock that a corporation, under its charter or articles of incorporation, is permitted to sell.

automatic teller machine (ATM).   An electronic machine, usually at a bank or savings and loan, that allows the use of a plastic card for making deposits or withdrawals of cash.

average annual yield.   The return each year on savings accounts of over one year. This will vary depending on the interest compounding method used.

average daily balance.   The average amount of money that an individual has on deposit on any given day.

back-end (or back-door) load.   A sales charge, usually relating to mutual funds, imposed at the time of withdrawal, usually decreasing over time; also called a "contingent-deferred" sales charge.

balanced fund. A mutual fund that maintains a balanced portfolio, generally 60 percent bonds or preferred stocks and 40 percent common stocks.

bankruptcy. The state of being unable to pay one's debts. Bankruptcy may be voluntary (the individual chooses to file for bankruptcy) or involuntary (the individual is declared bankrupt by a bankruptcy court).

bearer bond. A bond that is payable to the person having possession.

bear market. The condition of the stock market in which prices are declining or are expected to decline. *For contrast, see* bull market.

before-tax return. The interest, dividend and/or profit on an investment before applicable taxes have been paid. *For contrast, see* after-tax return.

bellwether security. A particular security that is seen as an indicator of a market's direction. In bonds, the 30-year Treasury bond is considered the bellwether; in stocks, IBM has long been considered a bellwether because so much of its stock is owned by institutional investors, whose trading actions tend to influence smaller investors and therefore the market generally.

beneficiary. The person entitled to collect the benefits of an insurance policy or for whose benefit property is held in trust.

benefits. Financial assistance received in time of illness, disability, unemployment or retirement from a medical or retirement plan, insurance or Social Security.

bid and asked. Price quotation for securities traded in the over-the-counter market.

big board. The board showing the current prices of securities listed on the New York Stock Exchange; generally, another term for the New York Stock Exchange.

blue chip. A term used to describe the highest quality stock or bond with minimum risk and satisfactory income or yield. Usually the issuing companies are nationally known, enjoy wide acceptance of their products or services, and have a history of paying stockholders a regular dividend.

bond. A certificate by which a corporation or governmental body promises to pay purchasers a specified amount of interest for a specified length of time and to repay the loan in full on the expiration date.

bond anticipation note (BAN). A short-term bond issued by a state or municipality that will be paid off with the proceeds of an upcoming bond issue.

bond basis risk. The propensity of a bond to lose market value when interest rates rise, and to gain market value when interest rates fall.

bond discount. The difference between the face amount of the bond and its current lower market price. *For contrast, see* bond premium.

bond fund. A mutual fund whose portfolio consists primarily of corporate, municipal or U.S. government bonds. These funds generally emphasize income rather than growth.

bond premium. The difference between the face amount of a bond and its current higher market price. *For contrast, see* bond discount.

bond rating. A system of appraising and rating the investment value of individual bond issues, with AAA as the highest.

break in service. The requirement in a pension plan that an employee work continuously for a certain number of years to qualify for a pension at retirement. A break in service can occur when an employee is fired, is laid off or quits and later returns to work for the same company.

broker. An agent, such as a stockbroker, who buys and sells securities, commodities or other property on commission.

bull market. The condition of the stock market in which prices are rising or are expected to rise. *For contrast, see* bear market.

buying on margin. The purchase of a security with part of the payment in cash and part by a loan, usually made by the broker.

callable bond. A bond for which the issuer reserves the right to pay off before maturity.

capital appreciation fund. A mutual fund that seeks maximum capital appreciation through techniques that involve greater than ordinary risk, such as borrowing money in order to provide leverage, selling short and high portfolio turnovers.

capital gains. Profit realized on the sale or exchange of a capital asset, such as property or securities.

cash dividend. That portion of profits and surplus paid to stockholders by a corporation in the form of cash. *For contrast, see* stock dividend.

cash management account. An account, usually offered by brokers, that allows you to invest part of your money and hold the surplus in a money market account.

cash surrender value. The amount an insurer will pay if a policy is cancelled before death.

cash value life insurance. Whole life insurance that, in addition to paying benefits in the event of death, acts as a savings plan to keep the premiums level during the lifetime of the policyholder. The owner can borrow against the cash value in the policy by paying the insurance company the annual interest rate established in the policy. At time of death, the face value of the policy will be reduced by the amount of any outstanding loan before payment to the beneficiary.

certificate of deposit (CD). A savings account in a bank or savings and loan association deposited for a fixed period and having a fixed rate of return, usually federally insured.

certified check. The check of a depositor upon the face of which the bank has stamped "accepted" or "certified" and thus guarantees payment.

certified financial planner (CFP). A professional who has completed a two-year course of study and passed required examinations and who qualifies for membership in the Institute of Certified Financial Planners.

certified public accountant (CPA). An individual who has satisfied the statutory and administrative requirements (differing in different jurisdictions) to be registered or licensed as such.

chartered financial analyst (CFA). An individual who has fulfilled the requirements of the Association for Investment Management and Research of completion of a particular curriculum and professional experience in the investment field.

chartered financial consultant (ChFC). An individual who has earned a professional degree requiring two years' of study and passing of college-type exams.

chartered life underwriter (CLU). A professional degree requiring two years' of study and passing of college-type exams.

closed-end fund. A specific type of mutual fund that operates much like common stock in that, once issued, the makeup of the fund is fixed and only the number of shares originally authorized can be sold. Closed-end funds, like stocks, are bought and sold on the stock exchange. *For contrast, see* open-end fund.

collateral.   Property that is pledged as security for a loan, to be forfeited if repayment is not made.

commercial paper.   Drafts, short-term notes, bank checks and other negotiable instruments for the payment of money; short-term, unsecured promissory notes with maturities no longer than 270 days, issued by corporations in denominations starting at $10,000, to fund short-term credit needs.

commission.   The amount paid to a broker or salesperson for selling property or securities, calculated as a percentage of the amount of the transaction.

common stock.   Securities that represent an ownership in a corporation and that participate in the profits by way of dividends after dividends have been paid to holders of preferred stock. Holders of common stock assume a greater risk but generally exercise greater control and may gain greater reward in the form of dividends and capital appreciation. *For contrast, see* preferred stock.

common stock fund.   A mutual fund that invests all or most of its assets in common stocks and that usually emphasizes growth.

compounding.   The payment of interest on interest; interest earned on a sum of money, which is added to the principal, with interest then paid on the larger amount. Compounding may be at various intervals, i.e., quarterly, monthly or daily. The more frequent the interval, the greater the total return.

compound interest.   Interest that is allowed to accumulate and that itself earns additional interest.

constructive dividend.   A dividend to which a stockholder has an unqualified right and which is therefore taxable, even though not actually received.

consumer credit.   Short-term loans to individuals for the purchase of consumer goods and services.

consumer price index.   A computation made and issued monthly by the U.S. Department of Labor that tracks the price levels of consumer goods and services.

contrarian.   A person who adheres to the theory that, no matter what the public believes will happen in the market, it will move the other way. Most stock market gurus who provide inside information on the market are contrarians.

contribution. The payment of a proportional share, such as a payment made by an employer to an employee's retirement plan.

contributory retirement plan. An IRA, TSA, 401(k) plan, thrift plan or other employer-sponsored plan in which the employee makes regular voluntary contributions from his/her pay.

convertible security. A bond, debenture or preferred share that can be exchanged for common stock or another security, usually of the same company.

convertible term insurance. A type of insurance that can be changed to permanent (whole life) insurance.

cooling-off period. A period of time in which a buyer may cancel a purchase, in most states three days.

corporation. A legal entity created under the laws of a state or nation composed, generally, of an association of numerous individuals acting as a unit in pursuit of a common purpose, such as a profit-making business. *For contrast, see* partnership, sole proprietorship.

"country" funds. Mutual funds that are invested in a specific foreign country.

coupon rate. The annual rate of interest, as a percentage of the face value, paid by a bond.

credit bureau. An establishment in the business of collecting information relating to the credit, responsibility and reputation of individuals and businesses and of providing credit reports to merchants, banks, etc.

credit card. A card or plate by which an individual can borrow money, either directly or, usually, by making purchases on credit.

credit line. The amount of money or merchandise a banker or supplier agrees to supply to an individual on credit, generally agreed to in advance.

credit rating. The evaluation of the ability of a person or business to pay debts, based on past performance and current obligations.

credit report. A document from a credit bureau giving a credit rating and financial data concerning a person or company.

credit union. A cooperative association that uses money deposited by a closed group of persons, such as employees of a company, and lends it to persons in the same group at favorable interest rates.

custodian. The bank or trust company that maintains a mutual fund's assets; an agent who provides the safekeeping of securities but has no role in portfolio management. Individual retirement accounts and Keogh plans require a custodian to maintain assets and make reports of changes in the account.

dealer. An individual or form in the securities business acting as a principal rather than as an agent. Dealers buy for their own accounts and sell to customers from their own inventory. Unlisted over-the-counter stocks are often bought and sold by dealers.

debenture. A note or bond that is backed by the general credit of the issuing entity and is not secured by a mortgage or lien on any specific property.

deferred annuity. An annuity in which payments are made or begun at a future time, such as when the annuitant reaches a certain age.

deferred compensation. Compensation that will be taxed when received, such as contributions by an employer to a qualified pension or profit-sharing plan on behalf of an employee.

deferred-interest bond. A bond that pays interest at a later date, such as a zero coupon bond.

defined-benefit plan. A fixed-benefit pension plan, paid entirely by the employer. It specifies the size of the benefit, usually in relation to the employee's most recent salary, and specifies when the benefit can be paid.

defined-contribution plan. A money-purchase retirement plan, paid by the employer, with the benefits to the retiring employee determined by the amount of money that has accumulated in the account. The employer is only required to make a contribution, not to provide a certain guaranteed benefit at retirement.

deflation. A contraction in the volume of available money or credit that results in a decline of the general price level. *For contrast, see* inflation.

demand deposit. Any bank deposit that can be withdrawn without penalty at any time, such as a passbook savings account. *For contrast, see* time deposit.

dependent status. The relation of dependent members of a family to its principal wage earner for purposes of collecting pension or Social Security benefits. Usually such benefits are not available to dependents until the worker who earned the benefits has retired.

depreciation.   The lessening of value of an asset because of age, use and improvements due to better methods; the write-off of such loss of value for tax purposes.

discount bond.   A bond that is selling, or was issued, at a dollar price below the par value. When interest rates rise after a bond is issued, the bond will trade at a discount because its current yield is below that of newly issued bonds.

discount broker.   A broker who only buys and sells stocks and bonds. Since they do not offer advice, make a market or help customers to buy and sell, discount brokers have cut normal commissions by as much as 75 percent.

discretionary account.   An account in which an investor gives a bank, broker or financial adviser the authority to make investment decisions on the investor's behalf, including selection, timing and price of buying or selling securities or commodities.

diversification.   The strategy of spreading investments among a range of different securities to reduce the risks inherent in investing.

dividend.   A payment made by a corporation to its shareholders, the amount of which may vary with the corporation's profits and the amount of cash on hand.

dividend yield.   The current annual dividend divided by the market price per share.

dollar-cost averaging.   The practice of investing a fixed sum at regular intervals in a particular stock, regardless of stock market movements. The investor acquires more shares in periods of lower securities prices and fewer shares in periods of high prices, thereby spreading his/her investment risk over time.

double tax free.   Said of an investment that is free of both federal and state income taxes, usually income or interest received from a municipal bond issued by the state in which the investor lives.

Dow Jones average.   A stock market performance indicator. There are three Dow Jones averages, one for transportation stocks, one for utilities and one for industrial stock averages. The most widely quoted is the industrial stock average, which consists of the price movements in the top 30 industrial companies in the U.S.

early withdrawal penalty.   The percentage of an account that is charged to the investor if he or she withdraws funds before the term of the account. With CDs, the early withdrawal penalty, imposed by the banking institution, is usually the difference between that originally stated and ordinary passbook interest. If funds are withdrawn from a retirement account or annuity before the individual reaches age 59 1/2, the IRS imposes an early-withdrawal penalty of 10 percent.

earned income. Income from labor, professional service or self-employment (wages, salaries, fees), rather than from invested capital (interest, rents, dividends). Earned income is the only source for investments in IRAs and Keogh plans.

earnings-based certificate of deposit. An insured certificate of deposit invested in real estate and guaranteed by the FDIC, the income from which is interest only without the possibility of appreciation.

earnings per share. A common measure of the value of common stock, computed by dividing the net earnings (after interest and prior dividends) by the number of shares of common stock.

Employee Retirement Income Security Act of 1974 (ERISA). A federal law, aimed at eliminating private pension abuse, that provided pension-plan insurance through the Pension Benefit Guaranty Corporation (PBGC) and that authorized IRAs for employees who were not covered by a retirement plan where they worked.

Employee Stock Ownership Plan (ESOP). A type of company ownership wherein the employees of the company own all of the company's outstanding stock and share in the company's profits.

equity fund. A mutual fund that is invested in stocks rather than bonds.

equity investment. An investment in stock in which the investor is at risk if the value of the company goes down.

estate. The extent of interest that a person has in real and personal property; an individual's total property, real and personal, at the time of death.

estate planning. The process of arranging for the disposition of an individual's estate so as to gain maximum benefit of all laws while carrying out the individual's wishes.

estate tax. A tax imposed on the right to transfer property at death. The tax is levied on the decedent's estate, not on the heir.

exchange privilege. The right to transfer investments from one mutual fund to another, generally within the same fund group, at nominal cost.

ex dividend. Stock that is sold "without dividend," where the seller, and not the buyer, has the right to the next dividend, which has been declared but not paid. When stocks go ex dividend, the stock tables include an "X" after the name.

ex-dividend date.   The date on or after which a purchaser of stock is not entitled to a declared but not yet paid dividend.

extra dividend.   A dividend paid by a corporation in cash or stock beyond what is regularly paid.

face value.   The amount stated on the face of a security or insurance policy; the value at maturity or death; the value upon which interest is computed.

Federal Deposit Insurance Corporation (FDIC).   An independent agency of the federal government, established in 1933, that insures up to $100,000 deposits in member banks and savings and loan institutions.

Federal Home Loan Mortgage Corporation (Freddie Mac).   A federal agency that purchases first mortgages, both conventional and federally insured, from members of the Federal Reserve system and the Federal Home Loan Bank system.

Federal Housing Administration (FHA).   A federal agency that facilitates home mortgages by insuring loans made by FHA-approved lenders on homes that meet FHA standards.

Federal Reserve Board ("The Fed").   A board of governors, appointed by the President and confirmed by Congress, that manages the Federal Reserve system and sets national monetary policy.

Federal Reserve System.   A network of 12 regional Federal Reserve banks and their 24 branches, to which most national banks belong and to which state-chartered banks may belong, membership in which requires adherence to certain standards and limitations.

finance charge.   Interest paid for the use of credit.

financial planner.   An individual offering financial planning services. While no particular education, training, expertise or experience is required, a professional financial planner is usually either a Certified Financial Planner, a Chartered Financial Consultant or a Certified Public Accountant.

financial supermarket.   A company that offers a wide range of financial services under one roof.

first mortgage.   A mortgage that, because of its senior position, has priority right of payment over any other mortgages. *For contrast, see* second mortgage.

fixed annuity.   A type of annuity in which the periodic payments remain the same. *For contrast, see* variable annuity.

fixed-income security.   A type of investment, such as a bond, where the return is stable over the term of the investment.

fixed-rate mortgage.   A conventional mortgage in which the interest rate is fixed and the monthly payment remains the same. *For contrast, see* adjustable-rate mortgage.

401(k) plan.   An employer-sponsored retirement plan in which the employee agrees to a "salary reduction" and that amount, plus, often, a matching contribution from the employer, is placed in a tax-deferred account.

403(b) plan.   A tax-deferred retirement plan sanctioned by the Internal Revenue Code for employees of public school systems and certain charitable and nonprofit organizations.

fraud.   Any device or scheme used to misrepresent, deceive or take advantage of another in order to deprive that person of money, property or a legal right.

fringe benefits.   Benefits in addition to an employee's regular salary or wages, such as paid insurance, profit-sharing, paid vacations, etc.

front-end load.   Sales charges applied to an investment, such as a mutual fund, at the time of initial purchase and usually deducted from invested funds.

garnishment.   Satisfaction of a debt out of the property or wages of the debtor.

general obligation bond (GO).   A bond issued by a municipality to finance public improvements, such as streets, water systems, schools, police and fire stations, to be repaid from general tax revenues. General obligation bonds are generally safer than revenue bonds. *For contrast, see* revenue bond.

general partnership.   The association of two or more persons for the purpose of carrying on a business as co-owners who are personally liable for all debts of the partnership. *For contrast, see* limited partnership.

Ginnie Mae bond.   A fixed-income, mortgage-backed security issued by the Government National Mortgage Association, an agency of the federal government that invests in home mortgages. The bond returns both earned interest and a portion of the principal in each monthly payment for the life of the bond, at which time the principal has been reduced to zero. Ginnie Maes can be purchased in mutual funds, investment trusts and in bonds in amounts over $25,000.

Glass-Steagall Act of 1933. A federal law authorizing federal deposit insurance and prohibiting commercial banks from owning brokerage firms.

Government National Mortgage Association (GNMA). The federal agency that issues "Ginnie Mae" bonds.

government securities. Treasury bills, bonds and notes issued by the federal government.

growth fund. A mutual fund with the prime objective of long-term growth of capital. It invests principally in common stocks with significant growth potential. *For contrast, see* income fund.

growth and income fund. A mutual fund in which the choice of securities is balanced between those likely to provide income (usually bonds) and those that are likely to appreciate in value (usually stocks).

guaranteed investment contracts (GICs). A kind of fixed-income savings account offered by insurance companies to employers for the investment of pension-plan money.

guardian. A person who holds the legal power and duty to take care of another and to manage that other's property and person.

hidden-loan fund. A mutual fund that appears to be no-load but that has a back-end loan on redemption. These funds often charge annual management expenses that are higher than average.

home-equity loan. A loan obtained by using the equity in one's home as collateral and structured as either a lump sum or a line of credit under which withdrawals can be made from time to time as desired.

immediate annuity. A type of annuity where the periodic payments begin immediately.

impound account. Funds that are collected from a mortgagor, usually monthly, and held for the payment of taxes and insurance.

income fund. A mutual fund in which the prime objective is to provide current income rather than appreciation. It tends to invest in stocks and bonds that normally pay high dividends and interest. *For contrast, see* growth fund.

index fund. A mutual fund that seeks to mirror general stock-market performance by matching its portfolio to a broad-based index, most often the Standard & Poor's 500-stock index.

Individual Retirement Account (IRA). A type of retirement plan available to employees who are not covered by qualified pension or profit-sharing plans. With an IRA, an employee can set aside a portion of income each year tax deferred until withdrawal.

inflation. An increase in the supply of money and credit relative to available goods, which causes a decrease in the value of money and a substantial and continuing rise in the general price level.

initial public offering (IPO). Stock issued by a formerly private corporation and offered for sale to the public. Such stocks entail a high degree of risk.

installment contract. A type of purchase agreement calling for periodic payments that include both principal and interest.

insurance. A contract whereby, for a stated consideration, one party (the insurer) undertakes to compensate another party (the insured) should a particular event occur, such as destruction of named property, injury to the insured or others, or death.

insurance premium. The amounts to be paid to an insurer for insurance protection.

insured. The person or persons covered under an insurance policy.

insurer. The underwriter or insurance company with whom a contract of insurance is made.

interest rate. The percentage of an amount of money that is paid for its use for a specified time, commonly expressed as an annual percentage rate (APR). For a bond, it is called the coupon rate.

International Association for Financial Planning (IAFP). A nonprofit professional organization with over 12,000 members in the U.S. who are subject to its code of professional ethics, located at 2 Concourse Pkwy., Suite 800, Atlanta GA 30328-5347, 1-404-395-1605.

international fund. A mutual fund that invests in securities traded in markets outside the U.S.

investment adviser. A person who advises others, for compensation, regarding the advisability of buying or selling securities.

investment company. A company that invests pooled monies from many investors. It tends to provide greater professional management and diversification of investments than most small investors can obtain independently. A mutual fund is an open-end investment company. *See* mutual fund.

joint and survivor annuity. A contract, usually in a pension plan, issued by an insurance company, that promises to pay a regular sum to the annuitant for his or her life and then to continue the payments for the life of the surviving spouse.

joint bank account. An account in the names of two or more persons who have equal right to it, generally with the right of survivorship.

joint policy. Insurance on the lives of both spouses for the benefit of the survivor.

jumbo certificate of deposit. An insured certificate of deposit with a minimum denomination of $90,000. Banks and savings and loan associations maintain a separate market for jumbo CDs and offer higher interest rates than on CDs of lower denominations.

junk bond. A bond issued for a high-risk endeavor that pays a higher than normal rate of interest. These bonds are generally issued by corporations of questionable financial strength or without a proven record of success. They tend to be more volatile and offer higher yields than bonds with superior quality ratings.

Keogh plan. A type of retirement plan available to self-employed taxpayers, who can make yearly contributions of up to $30,000 tax deferred.

leverage. An arrangement in which one can use a small investment, such as a down payment, to control a much larger investment.

life estate. A legal arrangement whereby the beneficiary is entitled to the use of and/or income from property for the duration of his or her life.

limited partnership. An unincorporated association in which there are one or more general partners, who manage the business and are personally liable for partnership debts, and one or more limited partners, who contribute capital and share in profits but who take no part in running the business and incur no liability beyond the amount of their capital investment. *For contrast, see* general partnership.

line of credit. A fixed limit of credit granted to a borrower, of which he or she may use a part or all over time but may not exceed.

Lipper Analytical Services, Inc. A firm, based in New York, that tracks the performance of mutual funds.

liquid assets. Cash, or assets immediately convertible to cash.

living trust. A trust, usually revocable, that operates during the life of the creator of the trust and that may offer certain advantages in estate planning.

load. The sales commission charged by a mutual fund.

load fund. A mutual fund that charges a sales commission at the time of purchase.

low load. The up-front sales commission, usually 3 to 4 percent, charged by a mutual fund (as contrasted with "regular" loads of 6 to 8 percent). *See also* load, no-load.

lump-sum distribution. Payment of the entire amount due at one time rather than in installments, often occurring in qualified pension or profit-sharing plans upon the retirement or death of a covered employee.

management fee. The fee paid to the investment manager of a mutual fund by the fund's shareholders, usually .75 to 1.5 percent of the average net assets annually. *For contrast, see* load.

margin. The down payment made to buy stocks; money deposited with a stockbroker by an investor so that he or she may use the broker's credit to buy securities. The balance of the purchase price, usually borrowed, is treated as a loan at prevailing interest rates.

marketability. The probability that property or securities can be sold at any time at a favorable price and terms. Wise investors check the marketability of an investment so that, if their needs change, they can sell quickly and easily at the market rate.

market order. The order given to a broker to buy or sell securities at the best available price.

money market account. A savings account at a bank or S&L that pays current interest on the money in the account.

money market checking. A checking account that pays current interest on the money in the account.

money market fund. A mutual fund that invests only in highly liquid securities, such as short-term notes and loans, and pays the current interest earned on those investments.

money order. A type of negotiable draft issued by banks, post offices, etc. and used by the purchaser as a substitute for a check.

Moody's Investors Service. One of the ratings services, specializing in bonds and insurance companies, located at 99 Church St., New York NY 10007-2701, 1-212-553-0300.

Morningstar. A firm, based in Chicago, that tracks the performance of mutual funds and variable annuities for other funds, money managers and investors.

mortgage-backed securities. Certificates backed by pooled mortgages, such as Freddie Mac or Ginnie Mae, generally issued in denominations of $25,000 or more and offering higher yields than Treasury bonds providing comparable liquidity and safety.

mortgage pool. A group of mortgages sharing similar terms, interest rates, maturities, etc., such as Fannie Maes and Ginnie Maes.

municipal bond. A bond issued by a state, county or city government or public agency, usually to raise money for municipal expenses or for capital improvements beyond immediate resources of reasonable taxation. Municipal bonds are free of federal income tax. *See also* general obligation bond; revenue bond.

municipal bond fund. A mutual fund that invests in a broad range of short, intermediate or long-term tax-exempt bonds issued by states, cities and other local governments.

municipal bond insurance. Insurance, purchased by the issuer or by the investor, that guarantees the payment of interest and protection in the event of default. The two major insurers are the American Municipal Bond Assurance Corporation (AMBAC) and the Municipal Bond Insurance Association (MBIA).

mutual fund. An investment company that raises money by selling its own stock to the public and investing the proceeds in stocks, bonds or other securities, with the value of the fund's stock fluctuating relative to the securities chosen.

National Association of Securities Dealers Automated Quotation (NASDAQ). An automated information network that gives brokers and dealers price quotations on securities traded over the counter.

National Association of Securities Dealers (NASD). An association of brokers and dealers in the over-the-counter securities business, it has the power to expel members who have been declared guilty of unethical practices.

National Credit Union Administration (NCUA). A governmental agency that insures credit union deposits up to $100,000 on the same basis that the FDIC protects accounts in S&Ls.

negotiable order of withdrawal (NOW account). In effect, an interest-bearing checking account.

net asset value. A term used in evaluating stock, calculated by deducting total liabilities from total market value of all assets; for stock appraisal purposes, the portion that stock represents in the value of net assets, including every kind of property and value, including good will and the corporation's value as a going concern.

New York Stock Exchange (NYSE). The largest securities exchange market in the U.S., based in New York City, also called the "Big Board."

no-load fund. A mutual fund sold directly by the mutual fund company where there is no commission or service charge imposed at the time of purchase. Investment in such funds is made directly with the mutual fund company, rather than through a broker or financial planner.

noncallable. Referring to a security that cannot be redeemed by the issuer for a stated period of time.

odd lot. An amount of stock less than the established 100-share unit of trading. There is an extra charge for odd-lot trading. *For contrast, see* round lot.

offering. An issue of securities offered for sale to the public or to a private group, generally of two types: primary, with the proceeds going to the company, and secondary, where the funds go to a person other than the company, i.e., stockholders.

overdraw. To write checks or otherwise draw funds in excess of that remaining in one's account.

override. A commission paid to a manager on sales made by subordinates.

over-the-counter market (OTC). A market that trades in stocks that are not listed on the major exchanges but are traded through a telephone and computer network of dealers. The quotes are offered as "bid" and "asked."

participating preferred stock. Preferred stock that, in addition to paying a stipulated dividend, gives the holder the right to participate with holders of common stock in additional distributions of earnings under specified conditions.

partnership. A voluntary contract between two or more persons to place their money, property, labor and/or skill into a lawful business; the association of two or more persons as co-owners of a business. *For contrast, see* corporation; sole proprietorship. *See also* general partnership, limited partnership.

passbook.   A document, often in the form of a small book, issued by a bank or savings and loan in which a customer's deposits and withdrawals are recorded.

passbook account.   A type of savings account, usually at a relatively low interest rate, permitting deposits and withdrawals of funds at any time.

penny stocks.   Low-priced issues of stock, often highly speculative, selling at a low cost per share, often less than $1.

pension.   A retirement benefit that is paid at regular intervals, usually monthly, with the amount based generally on the length of employment and the wages or salary of the employee.

Pension Benefit Guaranty Corporation (PBGC).   A federal corporation established in 1974 to guarantee basic pension benefits in covered plans of 25 or more employees when the company pension plan is terminated.

percent.   A means of calculating, such as for interest, based on a whole divided into 100 parts. Interest at an annual rate of 6 percent would, over a year's time, return 6 cents for every dollar invested.

personal identification number (PIN).   A number given to a depositor, which must be used along with an ATM card to operate an automatic teller machine.

pink sheets.   A daily publication for the National Quotation Bureau that lists the bid and ask prices of unlisted, over-the-counter stocks. *See* pink sheet stock.

pink sheet stock.   A thinly traded, usually quite risky, over-the-counter stock that has a narrow market and only a few dealers handling it.

points.   In real estate financing, a fee or charge collected by the lending institution at the time the loan is made, with one point being equal to one percent of the loan amount.

preferred stock.   A class of capital stock in which the stockholder is normally limited to a fixed dividend but has prior claim on dividends and on assets in the event of liquidation. *For contrast, see* common stock.

premium.   The amount by which a security is selling above its par value; the sum paid by an insured to an insurer as consideration for insurance protection; a bonus or reward for some act; a value higher than normally expected.

preretirement income. The last salary earned before retirement, used by pension plans to determine benefits.

price-earnings ratio (P/E). The current per-share market value of a given stock divided by the earnings per share for a 12-month period. (Example: a stock selling for $50 a share and earning $2.50 a share has a P/E ratio of 20-to-1.)

prime. The part of common stock on which the owners retain the voting rights and receive the dividends. *For contrast, see* score.

prime rate. The lowest rate of interest charged by a specific lender to its most credit-worthy customers for short-term unsecured loans, often used as a measurement for setting interest rates on other loans.

profit-sharing plan. A plan established by an employer in which some of the profits of the business are paid to the employees or are accumulated in a fund for their benefit. The employer has no obligation to make a contribution and will usually do so only when the company makes a profit.

prospectus. An official document, required by the Securities Act of 1933, published to introduce new securities to the public. It gives pertinent information about the company, explains what will be done with the money and provides important information to potential investors.

proxy. Written authorization for one person to act for another, such as that given by a stockholder to someone who will represent him/her and vote his/her shares at a stockholders' meeting.

purchasing power. The value of a unit of money or other asset measured by the goods and services it can purchase. Purchasing power increases when the same amount of money will buy more goods and services, and it falls when it takes more money to purchase the same amount of goods and services. *See also* inflation, deflation.

qualified retirement plan. A private retirement plan that meets the rules and regulations of the Internal Revenue Service, permits tax-deductible contributions and in which earnings are tax-sheltered until withdrawal.

rating. An evaluation of comparative quality or worth; a classification according to grade. In bonds, rating refers to the quality of the bond. The top grades are AAA (prime), AA (excellent) and A (high grade). In insurance companies, rating refers to the

company's financial condition. The top grades are AAA to AA−
(Standard & Poor's), A+ to A− (A.M. Best).

Real Estate Investment Trust (REIT).   A company, usually traded
publicly, that invests in real estate ventures in order to earn profits
for shareholders. Equity REITs invest in real estate; mortgage
REITs lend money to building developers.

recession.   A set-back or slowdown in the economic growth of a
nation, less severe than a depression, in which there is usually a
rise in unemployment and a slowdown in business activity.

record date.   The date on which is determined the "shareholders
of record" who will receive a stock dividend or capital gains
distribution, normally the business day immediately before the
ex-dividend date. *For contrast, see* ex-dividend date.

red herring.   A preliminary prospectus used to obtain an indication
of interest from the public in a new issue, so-called because of
the red ink on the cover.

regional fund.   A mutual fund that concentrates its investments
within a specific geographic area, usually the fund's local region.
The objective is to take advantage of regional growth potential.

registered representative.   A full-time stockbroker who is licensed
with an exchange to do business with the public, also known as
an account executive or customer's broker.

replacement ratio.   The difference between an individual's last
working salary and his or her income in retirement. For example, if the individual's last working salary was $25,000 a
year, and his or her retirement income was $6,250 per year, the
replacement ratio would be 25 percent. The replacement ratio
of Social Security benefits now averages between 21 and 33
percent.

return of capital.   Payments received by an individual that represent
all or part of his or her original investment and hence are not
taxable income.

revenue anticipation note (RAN).   A short-term debt issue by a
municipality that is to be repaid out of anticipated revenues such
as sales taxes.

revenue bond.   A municipal bond issued for a specific project to be
repaid solely from revenue produced by the project for which the
bonds were issued, such as tolls from a bridge. *For contrast, see*
general obligation bond.

reverse home mortgage. A mortgage taken on the equity in a home, the proceeds of which are used to provide a monthly income to the home owner, with the loan to be repaid when the home owner dies or the house is sold.

reverse stock split. Reduction in the number of corporate shares outstanding by calling in all shares and issuing a smaller number, although the capital of the corporation remains the same. The effect is to increase the value of each share. *For contrast, see* stock split.

revolving credit. Type of credit arrangement in which an individual can buy goods or borrow money on a continuing basis so long as the outstanding balance of the account does not exceed a certain limit.

rollover IRA. An IRA established to receive money rolled over from an employer's retirement plan. Any amount can be rolled over, but the rollover must be done within 60 days of receipt to avoid paying income taxes in the year you receive the money.

round lot. A stock transaction of 100 shares or multiples of 100 shares. A round lot does not incur special charges. *For contrast, see* odd lot.

score. The part of common stock on which the owners receive only the price appreciation. *For contrast, see* prime.

secondary offering. In securities, the offering for sale of a large block of stock by an investment underwriter that is not a new issue but one that has been held by the corporation or by a large stockholder.

second mortgage. A mortgage of property that ranks in priority below a first mortgage.

sector fund. A mutual fund that operates several specialized industry sector portfolios under one umbrella, with transfers between the various portfolios at little or no cost to the investor.

Securities and Exchange Commission (SEC). A federal agency, established by Congress in the 1930s, that regulates the trading of securities to protect investors.

Securities Investor Protection Corporation (SIPC). An agency established under federal law (but not itself a federal agency) to protect investors from loss if a broker goes bankrupt or goes out of business.

self-directed IRA. An individual retirement account that can be actively managed by the account holder. Usually, a setup fee is required, and an annual management fee is charged.

self-employed income. Income earned when an individual has his or her own business or is a partner in a business. Such individuals pay self-employment taxes to Social Security that are about double those paid by persons employed by someone else. Self-employed individuals are permitted to open Keogh plans and IRAs.

simplified employee pension plan, individual retirement account (SEP–IRA). A retirement plan primarily for self-employed persons.

single premium life. A type of life insurance policy, intended as an investment, in which the policyholder pays a single premium, gets a declining death benefit and earns income on a tax-deferred basis.

small claims court. A special court that provides for fast, inexpensive settlement of claims of small amounts.

Social Security. A federal program of retirement insurance under which employees, employers and the self-employed contribute to a special trust fund, out of which benefits are paid when the individual is retired or becomes disabled.

sole proprietorship. A form of business in which one person owns all the assets of the business and is solely liable for all its debts. *For contrast, see* corporation; partnership.

specialty fund. A mutual fund specializing in the securities of a particular industry or group of industries, special types of securities or regional investments.

split annuity. A type of annuity consisting of two separate contracts, one providing an immediate pay-out and the other a deferred annuity, the tax-deferred income from which effectively replaces the amount invested in the immediate annuity.

Standard & Poor's 500–stock index. The composite average of 500 stocks on the New York Stock Exchange expressed in the form of an index number, against which changes can be related.

state guaranty fund. A program existing in most states under which the state establishes a fund to protect policyholders should an insurance company fail.

stock. A right of ownership in the assets of a corporation; a share of stock represents an equity in the corporation, as opposed to notes or bonds that are not equities and represent no ownership interest.

stockbroker.   An individual who buys or sells stock as the agent of another.

stock dividend.   A dividend paid in securities rather than cash.

stock split.   Issuance of additional shares of stock that are then substituted for outstanding shares, for example, two-for-one, with no changes in the assets of the corporation. The purpose is to lower the market price per share to make for wider trading of the stock and, ultimately, an increase in value. *For contrast, see* reverse stock split.

stop-loss order.   An order given to a stockbroker to buy or sell certain securities when the market reaches a particular price, at which time the stop order becomes a market order, and the investment is sold as soon as a buyer can be found.

street name.   Securities held in the name of a broker rather than in the name of the actual purchaser are said to be held in "street name," frequently occurring when securities are bought on margin or simply for convenience.

surrender penalty.   A sales commission applicable when a purchaser, such as the holder of a single-premium life insurance policy, cancels the contract.

surrender value.   In insurance, the current value of a policy.

tax anticipation note (TAN).   A short-term obligation of a state or municipal government to finance current expenditures pending receipt of expected tax revenue.

tax credit.   A dollar-for-dollar reduction in an individual's tax bill.

tax deferral.   The delaying of a tax liability; the permissibility, under certain circumstances, of earning interest or other income and paying taxes at some future time.

tax-deferred annuity.   A means of accumulating fixed income upon which the income tax can be delayed until some time in the future when the money is withdrawn.

tax-free income.   Income that is exempt from state and/or federal income taxes, usually income from municipal bonds. *See also* double tax free.

tax shelter.   An investment, often a limited partnership, that provides tax deductions and/or tax deferral, usually sold to people in high-tax brackets who can afford to lose their money if the investment goes sour; a device by which an individual is able to reduce or defer payment of taxes, such as a real estate investment where depreciation, interest, taxes, etc. are offset against ordinary income.

tax-sheltered annuity (TSA). A particular type of tax-deferred retirement plan that operates much like an IRA but that is available only to certain eligible employees such a teachers or employees of a church or nonprofit hospital. In a TSA, the employee agrees to a "salary reduction" with that amount automatically deducted from the employee's paycheck and invested in an annuity or mutual fund, with income taxes deferred until withdrawal.

ten-year rule. A requirement under Social Security that a divorced spouse must have been married for at least ten years prior to the divorce to collect benefits on the work record of the ex-spouse. Such benefits can be collected only if the divorced spouse has not remarried.

thrift plans. An employer-sponsored savings plan under which the employee makes voluntary contributions and the employer matches the money according to a prearranged formula and the interest income or profits inside the thrift plan are tax deferred until the money is withdrawn.

time deposit. A bank or savings and loan deposit that is to remain for a specified period of time or on which notice must be given to the bank before withdrawal. Any withdrawal made before the agreed-upon date may incur a substantial early-withdrawal penalty. *For contrast, see* demand deposit.

total return. The income from an investment and any profit realized from its sale; the performance of an investment, including yield (dividends, interest, capital gains) as well as changes in per-share price, calculated over a designated period of time.

trail commissions. Payments to a sales representative (as of a mutual fund) for on-going services such as information and consultation.

Truth-in-Lending Act. A federal law requiring that persons applying for credit be given all relevant information as to the cost of that credit.

12b-1 plan. A mutual fund operating under a section of federal law that permits selling costs and promotion expenses of the fund to be deducted from the fund's assets.

U.S. Treasury bill.   A short-term obligation of the federal government. Treasury bills are issued for periods of 3, 6 and 12 months, and they are sold at a discount.

U.S. Treasury bond.   A long-term obligation of the federal government. Treasury bonds have maturities from 10 to 30 years. Also, a bond issued by a corporation and then reacquired.

U.S. Treasury note.   An obligation of the federal government with a maturity of one to five years, on which interest is paid by coupon.

utilities.   An area of stock market trading that includes gas, electric, telephone and other such companies regulated under federal and/or state law.

variable annuity.   A type of annuity that is invested by the insurance company in a portfolio of stocks or other investments that can rise or fall with the market and that therefore results in payments to the purchaser of varying amounts depending on the success of the portfolio. The purpose is to offset the deflated value of the dollar caused by inflation.

vesting.   The point at which an employee's right to collect future pension benefits becomes effective, whether or not the employee may in the future change jobs. Legally an employee must be 100 percent vested after 15 years' service. An employee can obtain specific information regarding his or her vesting in their summary plan description booklet.

whole life insurance.   Life insurance for which the premium remains the same and is collected over the life of the insured and which builds up cash value within the policy. Also called straight life insurance.

yield.   Interest or dividend earned on an investment, expressed as a percentage of its current market value; the proportionate rate that the income from an investment bears to the total cost, taking into consideration the time period of the investment.

zero coupon bond.   A bond that does not pay annual interest and that is issued at a discount price, with the return at maturity the compounding effect of the stated interest rate over the life of the bond.

INDEX

If you enjoyed Jim's book, you'll like his monthly newsletter, *It's Your Money!*

What's most important is not the amount of money you have but in knowing how to use the money you have, how to get the information you need, and how to develop a financial plan that will lead you to financial security.

Jim's prime goal in writing his monthly newsletter on personal finance is to help subscribers invest wisely and manage their money to their best advantage. *It's Your Money*, now in its twelfth year, has helped people all across the country to understand how money works and how to make the most of it all through their working years and well into retirement.

Drawing on his background and contacts on Wall Street, in Washington, in the media, and from his extensive research, Jim gives readers his best advice on saving, investing, planning for retirement, getting the best values in credit cards, air travel, and hotel accommodations, finding the highest interest rates, the best mutual funds, the safest tax-free investments, and more.

For information on how YOU can subscribe to *It's Your Money*, call

1–800–701–SAVE

Ask about our Introductory Rates.

Or you can write to
**It's Your Money, 810 Idylberry Road,
San Rafael CA 94903.**